Visions of Chimney Rock:

A Photographic Interpretation of the Place and Its People

Edited by Helen L. Richardson
Introduction by Dr. W. James Judge

A publication of the Chimney Rock Interpretive Association

Enjoy this virtual tour of Chimney Rock.
H. L. Richardson

WESTERN REFLECTIONS PUBLISHING COMPANY®
Montrose, CO

Chimney Rock is a place of importance to all Americans. The cultural features of Chimney Rock and the history they embody are non-renewable and irreplaceable resources protected by Federal law. We ask you to join us in our goal of preserving the past for the future by respecting the site. It is through our understanding of the past that we'll answer our innate questions about mankind's origins and what defines us as human.

Cover Art: An original watercolor created especially for this book by Pagosa Springs artist Denny Rose

© 2006 Chimney Rock Interpretive Association
Pagosa Springs, CO 81147
970/264-2287

All rights reserved in whole or in part.

ISBN-13: 978-1-932738-38-4
ISBN-10: 1-932738-38-X

Library of Congress Control Number: 2006925615

First Edition
Printed in the United States of America

Cover and text design by Laurie Goralka Design

Western Reflections Publishing Company®
219 Main Street
Montrose, CO 81401
www.westernreflectionspub.com

VISIONS OF CHIMNEY ROCK: A PHOTOGRAPHIC INTERPRETATION OF THE PLACE AND ITS PEOPLE

Edited by: Helen L. Richardson
Illustrators: Jean Carson
Dick Ostergaard

Contributing Writers:
Jennie Ferrell
Joanne Hanson
Sharon Hatch
Bill Hawthorne
Peggy Jacobson
W. James Judge
J. McKim Malville
Elizabeth Ann Morris
Dick Moseley
Alan F. Peterson
Glenn Raby
Ron Sutcliffe
Dick and Ann Van Fossen
Charley Worthman

Contributing Photographers:
Scott Allen, Mountain Snapshots
Bruce Andersen
Christie Calderwood
David Herrell
Jeff Laydon, Pagosa Photography
Dick Moseley
John and Helen Richardson
Anasazi Heritage Center
Laboratory of Tree Ring Research, University of Arizona
US Forest Service, Pagosa District
All photos of native people used with permission

DEDICATION
This book is dedicated to Jennie Ferrell and Peggy Jacobson, knowledgeable historians of the Ancestral Puebloan builders, Chimney Rock volunteers, and lovers of this place.

A PUBLICATION OF THE
CHIMNEY ROCK INTERPRETIVE
ASSOCIATION
Pagosa Springs, Colorado 81147
970/264-2287

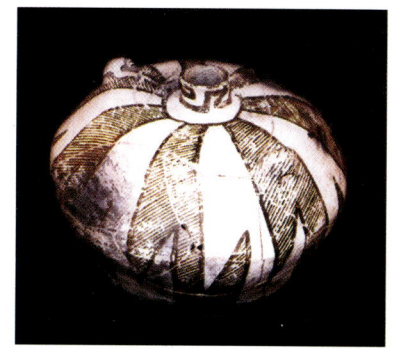

Photo by John G. Richardson

Table of Contents

Foreward vii

Introduction ix

Chapter 1 Chimney Rock, Colorado
    Then and now: A different era..2
    The people..4
    Early builders..8
    Why Chimney Rock?..10
    Ancient cultures...13
    The searchers..14
    Speaking of language 15
    Rock art..16

Chapter 2 Daily living
    Making a living 18
    Clothing and ornaments..20
    Tools and crafts...21
    Food and farming..26
    Living off the land 27
    Chimney Rock's useful wildflowers..29
    Tree fingerprints..35
    The search for water..37
    Transportation and roads...39

Chapter 3 The place
    The structures tell a story..42
    Tree rings tell the story...44
    The pit house 46
    Prayer plume holders..49
    The Great Kiva...51
    Father Sun..55
    The stone basin site..56
    Skywatchers..57
    Unexcavated sites 57
    Salvage site..58
    The ridge house..60

Pueblo trail pit houses 62
The guardhouse site 63
Behold the great house 65
Chacoan influence 68
Construction techniques 73
The twin kivas 75
Symmetry and asymmetry 77
The fire lookout tower 80
Room 8 81
Archaeoastronomy 82
Major lunar standstill 85
The departure 90

Chapter 4 The rocks
Nature at work 96
The spires appear 99

Chapter 5 Chimney Rock today
Plan for the future 104
Protect and study 106
Volunteers make it work 108
Return of native cultures 112

Acknowledgements 115

Bibliography 117

Index 121

Photo by Helen L. Richardson

Foreward

The Chimney Rock Archaeological Area is a treasure without parallel in the National Forest System. The site serves as a gateway for many travelers experiencing the archaeology of the American Southwest for the first time.

Even though only four major structures at Chimney Rock have been excavated and reconstructed, leaving most of this Ancestral Puebloan homeland preserved beneath the sandy soil of Southwest Colorado, the site has been heavily studied for decades. Scientists have developed several theories regarding the nature of the pre-historic community that evolved here. Questions abound regarding the purpose of this most distant outlier of the Chacoan system. Newer theories focus on Chimney Rock's possible role as a solar and lunar observatory. Set against the spectacularly beautiful southern San Juan Mountains, the site provides a natural calendar to track the movement of the sun and moon through the seasons.

While scientific types ponder the importance of the site, descendents of the former residents recognize the Chimney Rock Archaeological Area as a site of great spiritual significance. With sensitivity to modern-day Native Americans and in a partnership with the Forest Service, this unique site is protected and interpreted by a large team of volunteers who generously contribute their time, talents, and passion to welcome visitors and share their appreciation of the cultural richness of the southwest.

Chimney Rock inspires intellectual wonderment for the casual visitor as well as within the academic community. With these visitors in mind, this book has been created and published through the talents and commitment of volunteers who present the theories of various researchers illustrated with incredible photographs, capturing the awe-inspiring setting of this public jewel.

Jo Bridges

Introduction

All who have visited Chimney Rock acknowledge it is a very special place. This book presents an eclectic collection of subjects from archaeology to geology to history to the natural world of the Chimney Rock region. Of particular interest is the emphasis on the integration of the natural and cultural worlds expressed in the photos and the text. As a natural area, Chimney Rock is unmatched in diversity, and the beautiful images contained herein speak well to the inspiration it provides us.

Illustration by Dick Ostergaard

Chimney Rock mesa has been a special area to visitors for a very long time. Archaeological research shows its occupation at least as far back as the AD 800s. People evidently enjoyed the view then as much as they do now. But archaeological evidence also reveals its most intensive occupation during the Chaco florescence, from AD 900-1130. For the Chaco people then, perhaps Chimney Rock held an even deeper meaning. The complexity of the Chacoan culture is reflected in the complexity of Chacoan archaeology, which yields conflicting theories as well as unsolved, perhaps unsolvable, mysteries.

This book is very cautious in presenting a cosmological explanation of the Chacoan presence at Chimney Rock, noting that a number of other theories have been offered. Yet when considered in the context of the geographic placement of other Chacoan outliers (see page 68 for definition), the Chimney Rock location emerges as a singularly unique site. There is no question that of the myriad of possible cosmological occurrences, it is the moon that displays its stunning northern standstill position at Chimney Rock, rising between the two spires when viewed from the precise location of a Chacoan Great House there. Observations of this event by knowledgeable Chacoans in residence there could have provided the basis of a ritual calendar and guidance for planting, harvesting, and scheduling ceremonies. Communicating this knowledge to the ceremonial center at Chaco Canyon may well have served to integrate diverse cultural elements of the San Juan Basin during the 10th and 11th centuries. Certainly the precise location of the Great House at Chimney Rock lends credence to the role of cosmology in explaining the massive, and technically difficult, labor investment in architecture displayed there.

Images captured herein, and the accompanying text of this book, offer a comprehensive insight into both the complexity and the mystery of Chimney Rock. They make both the archaeology and its interpretation all the more interesting. If they succeed in stimulating the generation of ideas that might further explain the unique features found here, then this work will have served its purpose.

Dr. W. James Judge

CHAPTER ONE

Chimney Rock, Colorado

Visions of Chimney Rock

Then and now: A different era

To some, a mystical, magical aura surrounds southwestern Colorado's twin pinnacles, Chimney Rock and Companion Rock. Looking out from the mesa at the Rock's feet, present-day visitors marvel at the view that encompasses the fertile Piedra River Valley and reaches as far as Huerfano Mesa some sixty-five miles to the south in New Mexico. Those lucky enough to watch a sunset from the mesa top and then descend by the light of a full moon are enchanted by the silence and the feeling of oneness with the world. These feelings are as difficult to explain as the purpose of ancient structures on the high, dry mesa.

Early in the AD 900s, people moved to the Four Corners region where their culture reached its peak nearly a thousand years ago. The Ancestral Puebloans brought their culture to the high mesa they shared with the two stone pinnacles that give this unusual site its name. There are many theories as to why the people of Chimney Rock chose to live on this remote mesa. Perhaps, some suggest, the region was a frontier outpost or a source of natural resources for nearby people. Others suggest it was a remote religious retreat or a defensive fortress. And still others believe

Photo by Dick Moseley

CHAPTER 1: Chimney Rock, Colorado

the structures beneath the twin pinnacles were built as solar or lunar observatories or shrines. Most likely there will never be a definitive answer, but there will always be those who seek and wonder and wish they knew more about those ancient builders.

Illustration from Chimney Rock Volunteer Handbook

RESEARCH PRACTICES

Archaeologists use analogy in a variety of ways to explain the past. To figure out the unknown, they begin with the known. Analogy often is the best and sometimes the only way to explain the behavior of people who are not here to explain it themselves or explain it in an alternative way for a different view beyond that of the people themselves.

One of the ways to use analogy in archaeology is called ethnographic analogy. This means explaining the archaeological evidence in terms of behavior recorded in the historic and ethnographic record.

The advantage of ethnographic analogy is that human behavior in countless types of cultures all over the world has been recorded in ethnographic and historical documents. The disadvantages are that such records are, of course, always biased. Also, the culture you are investigating archaeologically may not be related to any known culture. Finally, history and ethnography do not include very much about material culture, which is what archaeologists are digging. The records might describe pyramids or clothing or houses, but not what the garbage looks like or where it is deposited.

(This material is excerpted from Nancy White's online Introduction to Anthropology course on MATRIX.)

Visions of Chimney Rock

Modern-day Hopi tribes believe their ancestors lived at what is now the Chimney Rock Archaeological Area.

Photo by Jeff Laydon

The people

The earliest people who inhabited the Four Corners area—the Paleo Indians of some 10,000 years ago—left little to tell their story. Surrounding the Chimney Rock mesa, a few of these early hearths have been identified by the spear and dart points abandoned when their occupants moved on, presumably to fresh hunting grounds.

The implements found at these Paleo Indian hearth sites differ in shape and style from those made by the people who came later. However, like the later people, they appear to have sought shelter from the elements. These hearths were sometimes snugged up against the base of a cliff and it makes sense to assume they used animal skins as shelters from the intense, high-desert sun as well as from the rain and snow.

CHAPTER 1: Chimney Rock, Colorado

It is assumed these earliest people were essentially hunters, surviving on their ability to kill the big game that roamed the region. As the climate warmed and large mammals became extinct—about 6000 BC—these

The Ancestral Puebloans made weapons and tools of stone.
Photo by John G. Richardson

people began a slow evolution toward more dependence on native vegetation. They gathered seeds, nuts, berries, fruits, and roots to supplement their diet of game.

Unlikely looking plants produced sustaining nourishment.
Photo by Dick Moseley

Early dwellers in the region made their living hunting available big game.
Photo by Christie Calderwood

Visions of Chimney Rock

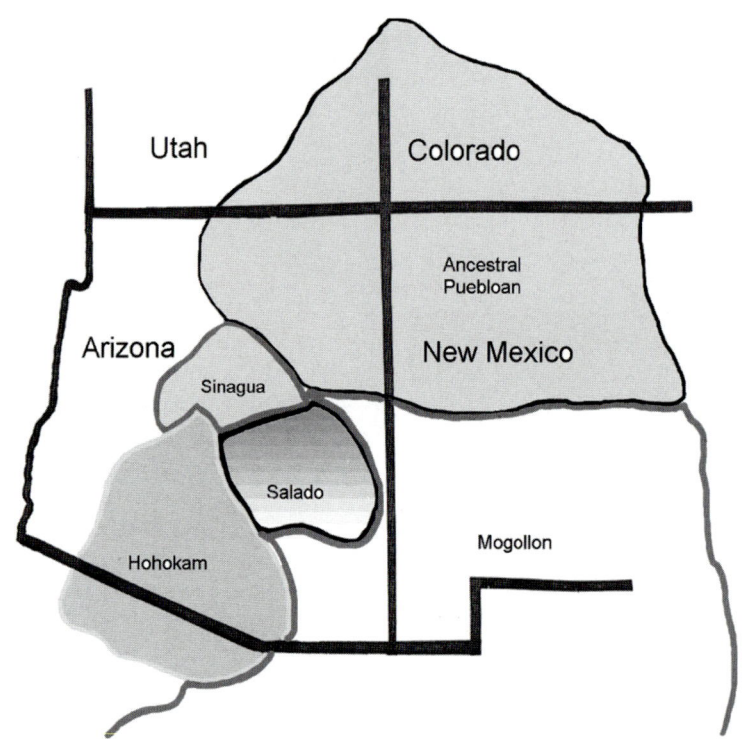

Prehistoric Cultures of the Southwest Desert Agricultural Phenomenon AD 950
Illustration from Chimney Rock Volunteer Handbook

ARTIFACTS HELP TELL THE STORY

Despite what's been uncovered so far by archaeologists, the disappearance of even a single piece of pottery can deprive everyone of important insight into the life and times of the Ancestral Puebloans who inhabited the site. For example, one piece of black-on-red Mimbres pottery has been uncovered at Chimney Rock. That unique style of pottery originated in southwest New Mexico, providing an important clue to trade patterns.

Items uncovered during excavations at the site are preserved at the Museum of Natural History, the Denver University Museum, and at the Anasazi Heritage Center in Dolores, CO.

CHAPTER 1: Chimney Rock, Colorado

By 1000 BC, the hunters relied less and less on hunting and gathering and began actually to cultivate small bits of land. They grew squash and corn, using techniques probably learned from their neighbors, the Hohokam and Mogollon. These two groups, in turn, most likely learned to grow crops from natives of Mexico, with whom they traded.

As cultivating crops grew in importance, the people of the Four Corners region—now labeled Archaic Indians—became less nomadic. Like modern-day gardeners, they needed to be near their small plots to pull weeds, irrigate, and keep away pests that would quickly eat or destroy the precious crops. Based on roles in modern-day pueblos, we assume these seasonal tasks fell to the women and children.

This 1000-year-old pot clearly demonstrates its coil construction.

Photo by John G. Richardson

Visions of Chimney Rock

Early builders

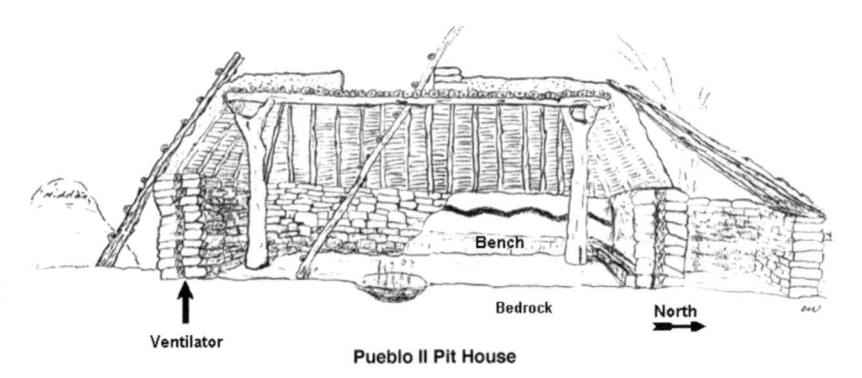

Pueblo II Pit House
Ventilator — Bench — Bedrock — North

Illustration from Chimney Rock Volunteer Handbook

With increasing dependence on cultivated crops, the former nomads stayed put for longer periods of time, necessitating improvement in the quality of their homes. Some of their earliest structures were built of rock. The next level of sophistication saw excavated pit houses walled and roofed with mud and sticks, a construction technique now called jacal or wattle and daub.

This lichen-covered rock is actually a fragment of jacal found at Chimney Rock.
Photo by Helen L. Richardson

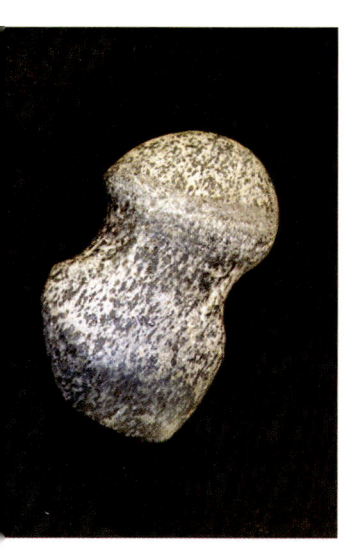

CHAPTER 1: Chimney Rock, Colorado

Tools fashioned from stone eased some tasks of daily living for ancient dwellers at Chimney Rock.
Photo by John G. Richardson

As early as 500 BC the people of the Four Corners area began a transition from this Archaic culture to one which archaeologists call the Anasazi (now replaced by the more accurate term Ancestral Puebloan). By AD 100, these industrious people left enough cultural artifacts to be identifiable as Basketmaker, a classification of early Ancestral Puebloans. As these people's culture continued to evolve, they built even more intricately constructed masonry structures.

As the diet improved in about 500 BC with the addition of beans to the already established maize and squash, the population exploded. By AD 700 to 800, the Ancestral Puebloans of the Four Corners area needed more land for farming to support their burgeoning numbers. It is assumed they moved steadily northeast in search of land on which to grow crops, and

Illustration by Jean Carson

These colorful beans are direct descendents of those grown in the Four Corners region nearly a thousand years ago.

Photo by John G. Richardson

9

Visions of Chimney Rock

came at last to the fertile Piedra River valley. The people who settled the Chimney Rock area moved up the Piedra River valley in a leapfrog fashion until they reached the high mesa overlooking the river—the highest elevation in which the growing season allows the maturing of maize.

Higher elevations such as the Chimney Rock mesa dependably added snowmelt to spring streams.

Photo courtesy of the US Forest Service, Pagosa District

Why Chimney Rock?

Archaeologists have noted that, between AD 700 and 800, populations throughout the Four Corners area began migrating from lowlands to higher elevations such as Chimney Rock. These scientists have come up with a number of possible reasons for the movement.

One theory suggests the Ancestral Puebloans sought the wetter climate of higher elevations to escape the erratic and extreme drought cycles of the lower southern part of the Four Corners region. During the end of the ninth century, the San Juan River was sinking to ever-lower levels and the surrounding countryside was drying up. The people who

CHAPTER 1: Chimney Rock, Colorado

Ancestral Puebloans likely found the Chimney Rock mesa thick [with P]onderosa Pine.
Photo by Jeff Laydon

[...] on farming would [have be]en forced to look [for] more dependable [water sources]. The Chimney [Rock mes]a, like many sites [where] the Ancestral [Puebloans] migrated, is near dependable wa[ter, the] summer rainstorms of the mountains.

Another theory port[rays] the Chimney R[ock] region as a supplier [of] natural resources such [as] timber for constructio[n] projects in tree-poor regions to the south. Pollen studies show that, once the Chimney Rock mesa top was inhabited, it was quickly stripped of its forest of pine and fir, but those most likely were used locally.

Much as it was a thousand years ago, the trail to the top of the Chimney Rock mesa narrows to a single, easily defended path.
Photo by John G. Richardson

11

Visions of Chimney Rock

Why cut trees on top of the mesa when there were trees closer to the river?

While pinon pine and Gambel oak may have been locally available, studies conclude they were not used as construction wood. Researchers cannot say for certain where the trees of Chimney Rock went. However, they can say that once the native forest was gone, the mesa remained bare and treeless for centuries. Today's forest of pinon pine, juniper, and sage is a later ecology more suited to the mesa's current hot, dry climate.

From Peterson Mesa, skywatchers witnessed the sun rising between the rocks.
Photo courtesy of the US Forest Service, Pagosa District

It's possible the ancient inhabitants of Chimney Rock chose to live on the mesa top because they feared some enemy. Certainly the large, complex structure atop the mesa, known as a Great House, could be defended effectively against raiders, but archaeologists have found no evidence of attacks. Perhaps the location and obvious strength of the site were deterrent enough.

CHAPTER 1: **Chimney Rock, Colorado**

The thick, high walls of the Great House may have been for defensive purposes.
Photo by Helen L. Richardson

One of the newest ideas about the "why" of Chimney Rock lies with the science of Archeoastronomy—the study of these early cultures' relationship with the sky. A few buildings at Chimney Rock appear to be aligned with and intended to celebrate events in the heavens. This is a common feature of most human cultures, and certainly the related cultures of Chaco Canyon (in northwestern New Mexico) and Mesa Verde (ninety miles west in Colorado) were keen observers of the movement of the sun, moon, stars, and planets. Perhaps Chimney Rock was a solar or lunar observatory.

Ancient cultures

At Chimney Rock, there is an identifiable local architecture and cultural style quite different from that of the thriving Chacoan culture nearly one hundred miles to the southwest. The Chacoan architectural pattern is

Visions of Chimney Rock

THE SEARCHERS

In 1921, museum curator Jean Allard Jeançon and a group of colleagues surveyed and made initial excavations at Chimney Rock. They discovered many mounds (the low, earth-covered remains of buildings) not only along the ridge on the mesa, but also below in the verdant Piedra River valley. Their attention was captivated, however, by the high mesa ruins at the foot of the two stone pinnacles.

For several years, Jeançon and Frank H.H. Roberts Jr. excavated and reported on the amazing buildings on this isolated desert mesa. As other archaeologists, including Dr. Frank Eddy, professor of anthropology at the University of Colorado, visited Chimney Rock and studied the remains, a basic outline of the ancient culture emerged. It was recognized that these people were of the same general cultural group as the Mesa Verde peoples and also shared some aspects of the culture at Chaco Canyon. It was an exciting time for archaeologists and led to identification of Chimney Rock's ruins as the Piedra Phase and Chimney Rock Phase of the Ancestral Puebloans.

View from ceremonial rock
Photo courtesy of the US Forest Service, Pagosa District

14

CHAPTER 1: Chimney Rock, Colorado

more complex than the small-house community of the native people of Chimney Rock.

The first settlers built round pit houses with thick walls of randomly laid stone and mud cement. These houses showed little concern for even courses and regular shaping of the stones. The local peoples' pit houses were individual structures, sometimes with adjacent towers.

With no written record of what the ancient Puebloans called themselves or their world, archaeologists have generally used the Navajo term Anasazi for this culture. Ancestral Puebloan is now preferred by modern-day Puebloans who claim decent from the ancient culture.

SPEAKING OF LANGUAGE

As Paleo linguists have studied evidence of pre-Spanish languages of the native people of the southwest, they suggest that the Ancestral Puebloans had several distinct languages and offer an idea of their origins. Most of these languages took thousands of years to form from intermediate and stock languages.

The oldest language, Keres, was spoken by the people living in the midst of the Ancestral Pueblos along the Rio Grande River. Recent research suggests the Zuni language is linguistically isolated. The Hopi language, on the other hand, is Ute-Aztecan and derives from the Piman and Shoshonean of the California area and earlier from the Numic and Central American Indians.

If we accept the oral history of the Tewa-speaking people and the Taos Day People, Chimney Rock inhabitants spoke Tewa and Tiwa, which are not mutually intelligible. Since they lived close together, we must assume they found a way to communicate.

Today, there are three known Tanoan languages and they remain distinct—not mutually intelligible by the Tiwa-speaking pueblos of today. Linguists trace Tanoan languages to the Plains languages.

Visions of Chimney Rock

Today, the Southern Ute reservation surrounds the Chimney Rock Archaeological Area. However, the tribe does not claim to be descended from the Ancestral Puebloans.

Photo courtesy of the US Forest Service, Pagosa District

ROCK ART

There is no evidence of any written language in the Ancestral Puebloan culture. While examples of petroglyphs and pictographs are common throughout the Ancestral Puebloan world, few petroglyphs have been unearthed at Chimney Rock.

While petroglyphs of this type are common throughout the Four Corners area, none have been found at Chimney Rock.

Illustration by Jean Carson

CHAPTER TWO

Daily Living

Visions of Chimney Rock

Twin kivas suggest the occupants of this community practiced dual governance.
Photo courtesy of the US Forest Service, Pagosa District

Making a living

Very little is actually known about the Ancestral Puebloan society. Based on the oral history of present-day people who believe their ancestors lived at Chimney Rock, extended families living together were probably based on lineal descent (lineage derived from either the father or mother or both). Dual governance is suggested by the presence of two great kivas in Chimney Rock's Great House, assuming they were contemporaneous. Under such governance, one kiva might regulate activities during the summer and the other during the winter.

The people most likely looked similar to today's Puebloans. Their general health was influenced by disease and poor nutrition, although they had abundant game to eat.

CHAPTER 2: Daily Living

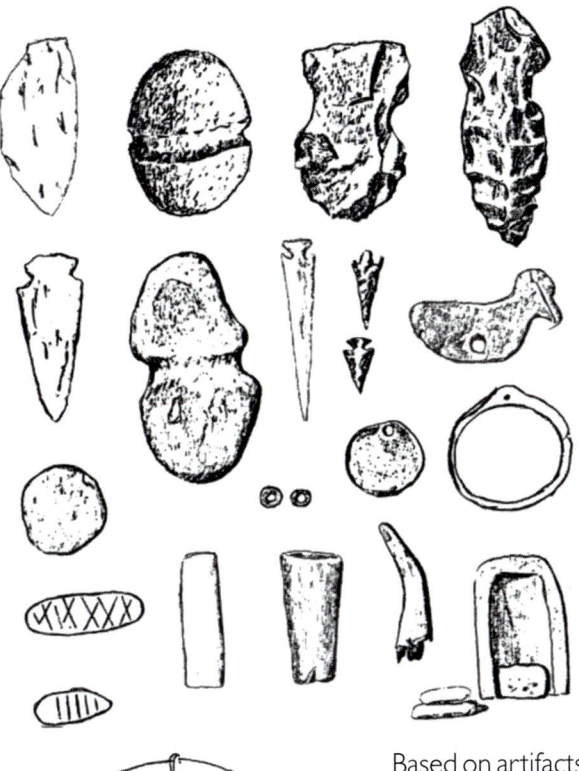

Stones were the building blocks for survival, making for hefty tools and implements.

Photo courtesy of the US Forest Service, Pagosa District

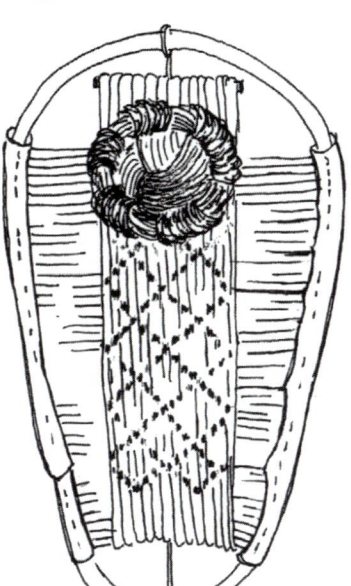

Based on artifacts found at Chimney Rock and other sites, everything the Ancestral Puebloans used was made of materials they found, caught, or harvested—materials such as stone, bone, clay, leather, sinew, wood, or fiber.

The most available fiber was from the local yucca plant. Beating the leaves between two pieces of wood or rock loosens the cellulose,

With a cradleboard, mothers could continue working while keeping infants safe.

Illustration by Jean Carson

19

which can be washed away. The long threads of fiber thus exposed could be woven, twisted, braided, and spun to make all manner of useful items, from blankets and mats to ropes, snares, even game nets and cradleboards. In fact, these clever people wrapped the soft down of turkey feathers and strips of rabbit fur around netting of yucca cord to make warm blankets.

Clothing and ornaments

Bracelet
Illustration by Jean Carson

In addition to textiles woven from spun yucca fiber, the Ancestral Puebloans fashioned clothing from animal hides and fur. They likely wore cloaks, kilts, leggings, and sandals. Beyond these utilitarian items, they are believed to have adorned themselves with pendants, necklaces, and bracelets made of stone and bone. Hairpins, pipes, and whistles have also been found, some trimmed with Pacific Ocean seashells.

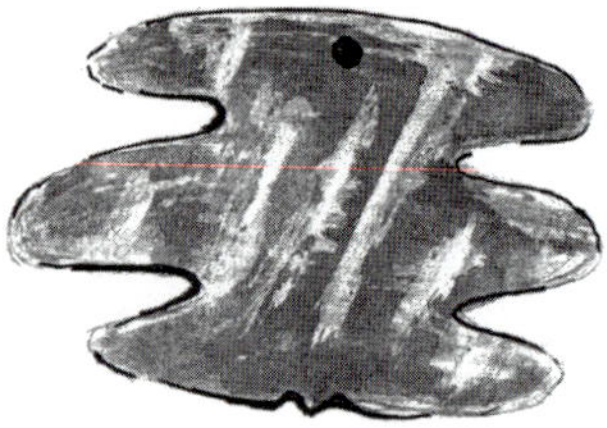

Abalone shell pendant
Illustration by Jean Carson

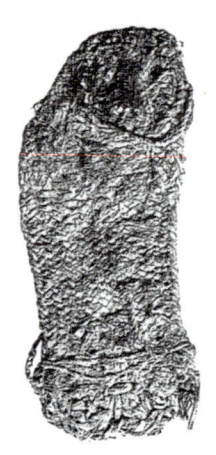

Sandals
Photo courtesy of the US Forest Service, Pagosa District

CHAPTER 2: **Daily Living**

Discoveries such as seashell ornaments strongly suggest the Ancestral Puebloans had their own long-distance trading networks with people to the West. In addition, colorful cotton cloth, copper bells, and macaw feathers seem to confirm they traded with the Indians of northern and central Mexico, perhaps through their neighbors the Hohokam, Sinagua, and Mogollon cultures.

Tools and crafts

Modern-day artists have painstakingly researched and recreated ancient methods of making black-on-white pottery.

Photo by L. Larason for the US Forest Service

As the Ancestral Puebloan culture evolved from the Basketmaker phases to the more sophisticated later phases, today known as Pueblo I, Pueblo II, and Pueblo III, they learned to finely grind clay from nearby shale slopes to make utilitarian and decorated pottery. Based on present-day practices, archaeologists believe women were the potters, creating their wares from coils of clay, shaped and pinched together, smoothed with

Visions of Chimney Rock

polishing stones, and fired in shallow pit kilns using wood-fueled fires.

The potters used mineral paints, carbon paints, and mixtures of the two to decorate the pots, producing black-on-white pottery distinctive to the area. One type of black paint could have been made from the Rocky Mountain beeplant, whose pollen is found in many of the area's prehistoric middens or trash heaps and in room deposits. Modern Pueblo Indians still use the beeplant with a mix of ground hematite (iron oxide) to make paint. And they continue to fire the decorated pottery in the low-oxygen atmosphere required to retain the black color.

The beeplant was the secret ingredient in the black pigment used to create black-on-white pottery.

Photo by Dick Moseley

Chimney Rock pottery is similar to that of Mesa Verde, but with differences researchers are still trying to identify. Of the several types of pottery that have been found at Chimney Rock, 90% of the recovered types are

These replica pots were made using the same techniques learned by the Ancestral Puebloans.

Photo courtesy of the US Forest Service, Pagosa District

CHAPTER 2: Daily Living

Coils of clay were used to fashion pots in a variety of shapes and sizes. These vessels, found during excavation of Chimney Rock, are stored at the Anasazi Heritage Center in Dolores, CO.

Photos courtesy of the Anasazi Heritage Center

Mancos Corrugated, Payan Corrugated, and Plain Gray types. Specific vessels found in the Chimney Rock area include a large corrugated grain storage jar.

Like modern-day people who keep the good china for special occasions, the Ancestral Puebloans may have used decorated pottery mainly for eating and for special ceremonies. The plain or rough-surfaced corrugated type was probably the everyday stuff, used for cooking and storage. Pottery was not limited to utilitarian bowls, jars, and mugs.

Visions of Chimney Rock

This large storage jar, found at Chimney Rock, is preserved at the Anasazi Heritage Center in Dolores, CO.

Photo by John G. Richardson

Excavations have also revealed effigies of animals and fanciful shapes, but their uses are not clearly understood. Perhaps the Ancestral Puebloans simply liked the decorative shapes.

In addition to their skill in pottery making, the Ancestral Puebloans crafted many types of implements from the substances of field and forest. Grass and twigs were used to make brooms. They wove baskets from yucca fiber and floor mats from grass, yucca fibers, and juniper bark. Yucca and bark fibers were also woven into rope and cording.

The Ancestral Puebloans recognized that game animals had utility beyond their role as food source. Splintered

These artifacts are part of the Chimney Rock collection at the Anasazi Heritage Center in Dolores, CO.

Photos by John G. Richardson

CHAPTER 2: Daily Living

bones became sewing needles. They also used bone or stone to make drills, scrapers, and polishers. Wood and stone provided raw materials for digging and planting sticks, hammers, axes, arrow and spear points, and milling stones (metates and manos) for grinding maize.

Corn and beans ground with a mano and metate cooked quickly, but contained unhealthy levels of sandstone grit.

Photo by Helen L. Richardson

The milling stones also could be used to grind beans into flour or simply to crush them for faster cooking. Even without crushing, Anasazi beans from ancient stock are sweeter and faster to cook than today's cultivated varieties.

All these needs and skills—grinding beans and corn into flour, tending crops, making all the clothing, blankets, hunting equipment, and tools needed to sustain life—add up to a work-intensive daily life for the Ancestral Puebloans.

Visions of Chimney Rock

Food and farming

Beans and corn were staples of the prehistoric diet.
Photo by L. Larason for the US Forest Service

Even as these early inhabitants of Chimney Rock became an agricultural people who cultivated maize and beans, they continued hunting and gathering. But cultivated crops obviously improved their standard of living.

In the region of Chimney Rock, farming plots were typically located near the Piedra

The Piedra River provided a somewhat erratic source of water for crops and daily use.
Photo by Dick Moseley

26

CHAPTER 2: Daily Living

River and its tributary streams. They grew their crops close to water for irrigation. However, a few dry-land plots were spread around the lower slopes of the mesa. In a land where both soil and rainfall were precious, the inventive Ancestral Puebloans appear to have built stone check dams across small drainages to keep the fertile soil from eroding and to trap rain water. These made for small but productive garden plots.

No beasts of burden to pull the plow for these hardy folks. They planted with wooden digging sticks, then carefully watered and weeded to get the most from each tiny plot. Brush fences helped keep the local wildlife from eating the precious crops, but the only sure way to save the corn and beans for people was to keep a close watch on the garden. This tiresome task would have been the duty of everyone in the family, from children to grandparents.

The mesa top provided a growing season long enough to mature maize for seed purposes.

Maize required eighty days of frost-free growth to mature and that's about the average frost-free period available at the 7,000-foot-elevation Piedra River Valley. However, this average means half of the time maize would not mature sufficiently to be useable seed corn for the following year. Without mature seed corn, and no local co-op source, farming comes to a halt. That lends credence to the suggestion that the many dry-land farm plots found on higher sites on the mesa—with more sun and longer frost-free growing time—were possibly the seed beds, used to assure mature maize for future planting.

Living off the land

In more southern areas where the populations relied heavily on agriculture for subsistence, the fluctuating climate created fat- and lean-year cycles that could have been difficult. However, the people of Chimney Rock were not totally dependent on cultivated crops. The biologically rich mountain zone yielded a variety of wild foods and game to supplement their cultivated crops.

Visions of Chimney Rock

Live ponderosa pines provided shelter for understory plants while dead ones harbored wildlife.

Photo by Jeff Laydon

Many species of plants share the mesas and valleys, ranging from the grasses and shrubs of open meadows to the serviceberry and wild currant in the shadowed understory of the conifer forests to the yucca and prickly pear cactus of the desert-like mesa top. Wildflowers and their fruits and seeds were abundant throughout spring and summer.

Pollen studies indicate the Ancestral Puebloans of the Four Corners region probably enjoyed many wild food sources. They likely ate beeweed, chokecherry, prickly pear cactus, serviceberry, banana yucca, Indian ricegrass, snowberry, sunflowers, cholla cactus, and pine nuts. Although pinon nuts and acorns were locally available and were commonly harvested in nearby Ancestral Puebloan sites, there is little evidence the people of Chimney Rock ate them.

CHAPTER 2: Daily Living

CHIMNEY ROCK'S USEFUL WILDFLOWERS

Perhaps no other plant at Chimney Rock has as many uses as the **Banana Yucca**. It was most likely the single most important wild plant to the Ancestral Puebloans who lived on this unique site. The tough, long fibers of the yucca leaves were used to make twine, rope, sandals, and sleeping mats. The flowers and sweet fruits were often eaten and may have been an important part of their diet. The large fleshy root was the main source of soap. When pounded, the saponin in the root produces a frothy suds that can be used as a hair shampoo or for other cleaning jobs around the hearth.

Banana Yucca
Photo by Dick Moseley

Rabbitbrush, also known as Chamisa or False Goldenrod, is one of the West's most spectacular fall blooming shrubs. Its dense yellow clusters of goldenrod-like flowers decorate the hillsides

Rabbitbrush
Photo by Dick Moseley

of Chimney Rock from late August through early October. It is often seen growing along roadsides and in disturbed areas. Some modern day Puebloan people use its flexible, slender branches for basket making, but the Ancestral Puebloans used it primarily as a fuel. The flowers and stems are used today by the Navajo and Hopi to make yellow and green dyes.

Cliff Fendlerbush, also known as Wild Mock-Orange, is the beautiful, white-flowered shrub that adorns the rocky slopes of the high-mesa in May and early June. When in blossom, it is the most prominent of our spring blooming shrubs. The four-petaled flowers are nearly an inch wide and produce a narrow brown capsule-like fruit that the Ancestral Puebloans scorned as a food source. The stems, however, were valued—they were used to make arrow shafts, planting sticks, and awls.

Chokecherry grows along Chimney Rock's roadsides, trails, and on its shady hillsides. The small bushy tree is best identified in late spring when its branches have long,

Cliff Fendlerbush
Photo by Dick Moseley

Chokecherry
Photo by Dick Moseley

CHAPTER 2: Daily Living

cylindrical clusters of five-petaled white flowers that may be up to five inches long. A member of the rose family, its fruits are bitter cherries that are better for cooking than eating raw. The fruits were probably gathered as a food by the Ancestral Puebloans and were sun-dried, then cooked with cornmeal or added to other flours to make a fruit bread. The bark of the Chokecherry tree has been used to make a cough medicine and the bark of its roots was used to make a purple-brown dye.

*Claret Cup Cactus
Photo by Dick Moseley*

Of the five cactus species that occur at Chimney Rock, the **Claret-Cup** is perhaps the most beautiful. The bright, cardinal-red flowers are shaped like small wineglasses. Although their fruits are smaller than the Prickly Pear Cactus, they are sweeter and some consider them tastier. Many modern tribes eat them and it's likely they were collected and eaten by the Ancestral Puebloans as well.

*Simpson's Ball Cactus
Photo by Dick Moseley*

The little round **Simpson's Ball Cactus** is easily overlooked as you walk the Chimney Rock trails since it grows close to the ground

Visions of Chimney Rock

among the sagebrush, pinon, and juniper. The round, ball-like plant is most obvious when its bright pink flowers are in bloom in mid-summer. The plants at Chimney Rock are unusual since those of the western slope are usually yellow flowered, while the ones on the eastern slope are normally pink flowered.

Wyoming Paintbrush
Photo by Dick Moseley

One of two species of paintbrushes that occur on this site, **Wyoming Paintbrush** is the tallest and latest to bloom, usually flowering in late July and August. It is normally branched and grows primarily with the sagebrush, pinon, and juniper. The plant is identified by its narrow leaves and three-lobed leafy bracts, which occur under the widely spaced flowers. The tubular flowers are green and extend beyond the bright red colored bracts.

A member of the snapdragon family, **Firecracker Penstemon's** bright scarlet-red, tubular flowers are a beautiful sight in mid- to late summer along the upper trail at Chimney Rock. The plant was named for its five stamens. Although it may have been used by the Ancestral Puebloans, it is better known as a life medicine of the Navajos, that is, it was used for a variety of ailments to induce healing. It can be used as a poultice to reduce swellings and on gun and arrow wounds; for coughs, stomach

Firecracker Penstemon
Photo by Dick Moseley

CHAPTER 2: Daily Living

problems, and burns; and for menstrual pain. The plant is also known as Scarlet Penstemon, Beardtongue, and Red Penstemon.

One of the most abundant plants growing along roadsides and in disturbed sites during mid- to late summer is the **Common Sunflower** or Annual Sunflower as it is sometimes known. This plant—considered a weed by many—was an important food source to the Ancestral Puebloans. Its seeds were eaten whole or ground and mixed with other grains such as corn to make cakes. The yellow flowers were used to make yellow dyes and the outer seed coatings produced dark red to purple dyes. The Common Sunflower is the state flower of Kansas.

Sunflowers
Photo by Helen L. Richardson

Snowberry is perhaps best identified in late summer when it's in fruit. The bright, glossy-white fruits are slightly larger than peas and give the plant its name. The shrub is a member of the Honeysuckle family and has opposite leaves with smooth edges and pink tubular flowers, which hang below the leaves. Although the fruits are reported to be edible by some sources, they are not very good and are mildly poisonous if eaten in large quantities.

The plant is used by some modern tribes as a minor medicinal plant in the treatment of sore throats, colds, and stomach problems.

The **Cane Cholla** is the largest native cactus at Chimney Rock. Its bright magenta flowers

Cane Cholla Cactus
Photo by Helen L. Richardson

33

Visions of Chimney Rock

are spectacular when blooming in mid-summer on top of the ridge. The spineless edible fruits remain on the cactus all winter and its seeds are known to have been an important part of the diet in Ancestral Puebloan times. However, the Navajo of modern times consider it inedible. They do not eat any part of this Cholla, which is also called the Tree Cholla, Candelabra Cactus, and Walkingstick Cholla.

One of the most common grasses at Chimney Rock, and the easiest to identify, is **Indian Rice Grass.** Also known as Indian Millet, this grass grows in large clumps and produces small black seeds that mature in June. Ricegrass seeds were a staple of the Ancestral Puebloans and can be used to make bread, cakes, or a hot cereal. Many modern tribes continued to use this important plant as a part of their diet up until the late 1800s. The dense clumps of this grass and their unusual fruiting heads are a common sight along the upper trail leading to the Great House Pueblo.

Juniper (left) and pinon pine (right) are relatively recent additions to the Chimney Rock mesa top.

Photos by Dick Moseley

CHAPTER 2: Daily Living

Photo by Bruce Anderson

Abundant animal life still populates the area surrounding Chimney Rock.

Photo by Christie Calderwood

Even though pinon pine and juniper are now growing high on the Chimney Rock mesa top, that's a reversal of the natural zone for these species. The ponderosa pine typically grows at an elevation of 4,000 to 9,000 feet, with the pinon growing in the lower range of that zone. It is difficult to explain exactly what caused this reversal.

Pollen studies of the mesa area show all three tree types were present at the time of prehistoric occupation. Two possible theories could explain the change. One theory suggests the prehistoric people used up all the local wood, clear-cutting the forest. After they left the area, only pinon and juniper were able to grow on the cleared—and consequently hotter—mesa top. Another theory is that a drought killed the thirsty ponderosa pine and allowed the dry-climate pinon and juniper to replace it.

TREE FINGERPRINTS

Someday scientists may be able to tell if trees from the region of Chimney Rock were cut and shipped south or were simply consumed by the Chimney Rock community. Using chemical fingerprints in the wood and soil of several sites, scientists are developing the ability to trace logs back to their place of origin.

Visions of Chimney Rock

In spite of the change in local forest tree types, the animal population of the Chimney Rock area remains similar to that of 1,000 years ago. During studies of the Chimney Rock sites, the remains of some thirty-four types of animals were identified including elk, mule deer, mountain sheep, wolf, coyote, mountain lion, bobcat, turkey, and porcupine, as well as several species of squirrel, rabbits, birds, lizards, fish, and snakes. Except for the wolf, these animals are still common in the Chimney Rock area today.

Archaeologist Frank Eddy suggests 90% of the wild meat harvest would have been the large hooved animals. During the early Basketmaker period, the weapon of choice for bringing down these game animals was the atlatl—a device that increased the force of a thrown spear. By approximately AD 600—the Basketmaker II period—the bow and arrow gradually replaced this weapon. Individual hunters used traps and snares, and it's likely groups cooperated to drive animals into yucca fiber nets, then kill the trapped quarry with wooden clubs.

Chimney Rock volunteer Ed Funk demonstrates throwing a spear using an atlatl.

Photo by Helen L. Richardson

On the home front, the Ancestral Puebloans enjoyed the company and utility of domesticated dogs and turkeys. Some researchers believe dogs were both pets and helpers on the hunt, while turkeys, kept in brush pens, may have been used as guard animals against intruders. Turkey feathers were used with yucca fibers and skins to fashion robes and blankets. Both

Turkeys were domesticated but may have been eaten only during hard times.

Photo by Christie Calderwood

CHAPTER 2: Daily Living

dogs and turkeys were eaten, but it's not known if they were daily fare or only consumed in times of dire need.

The search for water

More than anything else, water was a limiting factor in the Chimney Rock culture. Eddy theorized the people used closed-mouth clay jars, now known as ollas, to carry water from the Piedra River to their dwellings on the high mesa—a distance of two miles and a climb of 1,000 feet. Jars were undoubtedly used to trap rainwater, and snow could have been collected and melted in winter. There is some evidence of checkdams and reservoirs located below probable springs on the mesa. However, Eddy believes the river was the only reliable water source in summer.

The Ancestral Puebloans probably used these water bottles to transport water from the river to the mesa top.
Illustration by Jean Carson

During summer, storms threaten frequently, but they tend to bypass the mesa top.
Photo courtesy of the US Forest Service, Pagosa District

It may be that neither rain nor snow supplied water to those living on the mesa top because of an oddity reported by Jeançon and Roberts in their early published notes. Rainstorms seem to avoid the mesa top, many times rolling past to the north or south instead, sometimes almost touching the cliffs at the mesa's edge but rarely raining on the mesa itself. This

37

Visions of Chimney Rock

curious phenomenon also has been noted by modern visitors to Chimney Rock. Some theorize the rock spires form a type of windbreak.

Rain was and still is a rarity on the Chimney Rock mesa.

Photo by Jeff Laydon

Rumor has it there was once a spring somewhere atop the mesa near the pueblo. Oral history going back to the 1950s supports the existence of a small spring and dams. In the 1920s, Jeançon and Roberts searched in vain for a water source on the mesa top. Little if any evidence exists today and it is geologically very unlikely a spring of any significant value could have existed on this high tableland. However, Jeançon's early study of the area revealed at least six dams for storing water in drainages, and these dams and possible springs may have provided sufficient water for the people on the mesa.

CHAPTER 2: Daily Living

Transportation and roads

Water wasn't the only resource that had to be carried to the mesa top to sustain life. The Ancestral Puebloans had no beasts of burden or wheeled carts, so food and tools and all other needs had to be borne by people on foot. For carrying heavy loads, they made cone-shaped woven baskets used as backpacks, with perhaps a woven rope across the forehead for additional support.

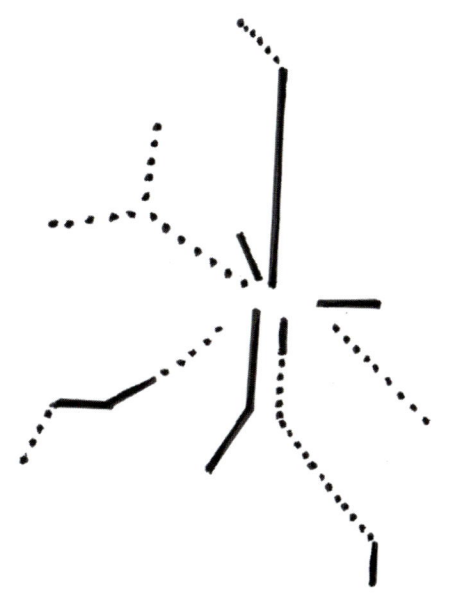

Today, the trail to the mesa top at Chimney Rock is a rough and rocky climb. There is slim evidence the Ancestral Puebloans had it any better. While the thriving culture in Chaco Canyon developed an extensive system of roads that radiated out from Chaco Canyon, no identified remnants of roads or stairways have been found in the Chimney Rock region, even though it is considered an outlier of the culture. The Chacoan roads were sophisticated constructions running rather straight and sometimes as wide as a county road today. Formally prepared paths, walkways, and stairways were common as well. These roads may have

An extensive system of sophisticated roads radiated from Chaco Canyon and its outliers.
Illustration by Jean Carson

Humans carried everything needed on the mesa top, possibly in baskets of this type.
Illustration by Jean Carson

39

Visions of Chimney Rock

been purely ceremonial to their Ancestral Puebloan builders, or they may have been crucial links between settlements, used for trade, travel, and communication.

While some Chacoan roads were elaborate and some were little more than footpaths, they all bore common features. They featured berms of loose rock on each side of the roadway, broken ceramics along the roadside, sandstone pavement, stair steps in canyon walls and cliff faces, and earth platforms and scaffolding to scale cliff faces.

There is a possibility this trail once might have been a Chacoan road. Photo courtesy of the US Forest Service, Pagosa District

Although no road segment has been found at Chimney Rock, in 1921 Jeançon and Roberts noted the discovery of a carefully prepared sandstone pavement, possibly once covered with mud plaster, leading up to the Guardhouse site near the top of the Great Pueblo trail. Little of it remains today but it leads to speculation: Was this the end of a road leading from Chaco Canyon to Chimney Rock?

CHAPTER THREE

The Place

Visions of Chimney Rock

The structures tell a story

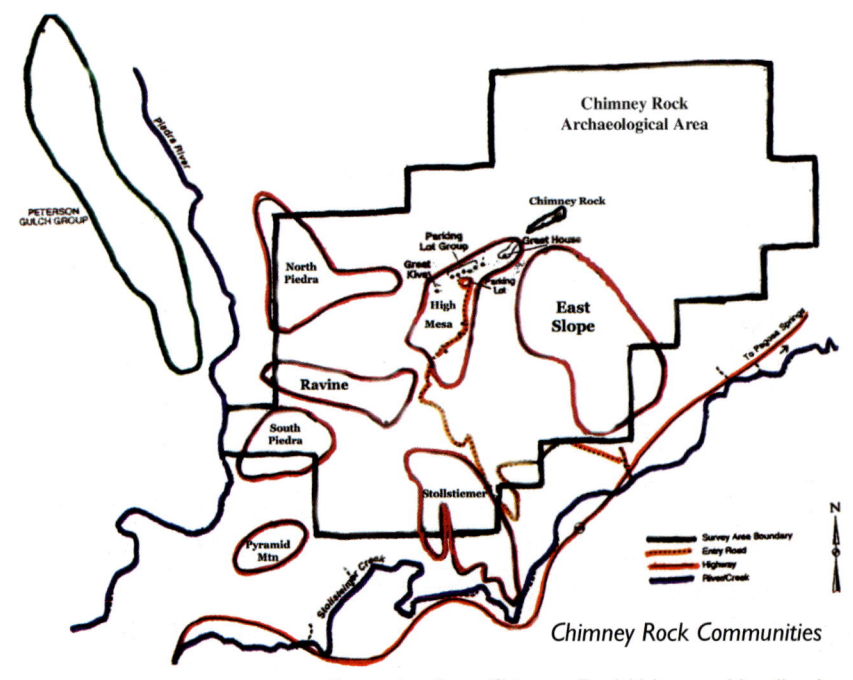

Illustration from Chimney Rock Volunteer Handbook

The exact relationship of the people of Chimney Rock to the Chacon culture remains a mystery. However, the legacy of structures the Ancestral Puebloans built at Chimney Rock partly tells their story. This legacy has lasted for more than 1000 years.

We can be quite confident of the age of the structures at Chimney Rock thanks to scientific dating methods based on tree rings, pottery styles, and stratigraphy—digging through trash heaps and assuming something buried by natural processes is older than the material that lies above it. All these methods support each other and yield fairly consistent results at Chimney Rock. Although there are Ancestral Puebloan ruins in the Chimney Rock region that date back to at least AD 600, all the excavated and stabilized structures on the Chimney Rock Mesa appear to have been built between AD 950 and 1125.

CHAPTER 3: The Place

The ancient people of Chimney Rock were prolific builders. Researchers have counted four hundred possible residences, thirty-six great kivas, and remnants of twenty-seven summer work camps near probable farm areas. .

The earliest Chimney Rock residence ruins are on a bench along the Piedra River. The houses are on the surface or slightly sunken and built on a base of rocks made round and smooth by the tumbling action of the river. The square-cornered structures were created with a lot of poles stuck into the ground, then interwoven with branches and grass and mudded over (researchers have dubbed it jacal construction). Over all, a flat roof was made of poles and branches and another heavy layer of mud. Unlike later structures, these houses had a walk-in doorway. Many of the houses were built with common walls and formed a line or an "L" shape. Most of the early Chimney Rock people lived in these jacal houses with a kiva nearby.

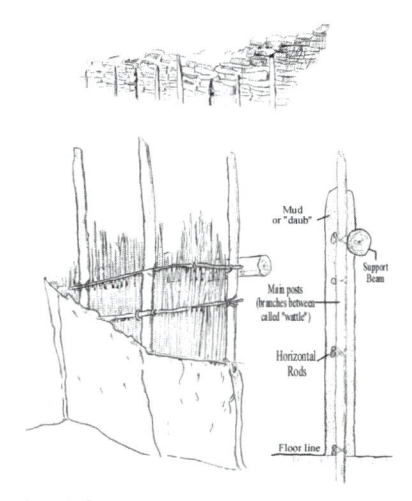

Jacal Construction
Illustration from Chimney Rock Volunteer Handbook

A quarter of the prehistoric residences at Chimney Rock were built on the high mesa. Of these, only three house structures—the Pit

Today's reconstructed Great House is a popular site for visitors to Chimney Rock.
Photo by Helen L. Richardson

Visions of Chimney Rock

House, the Ridge House, and the Great House—have been excavated and stabilized. Two others—the Salvage Site and the Guardhouse—were excavated, then partially backfilled with dirt to prevent further erosion or collapse. The Great Kiva on the high mesa was also excavated and stabilized.

TREE RINGS TELL THE STORY

Researchers use the principle of stratigraphy to establish relative ages of buried objects. Pottery styles, which change over time, are also reliable indicators of relative age. Neither of these methods can tie an object or event to a specific year; they can only establish that one thing may be older than another. The most accurate dating method for Chimney Rock researchers has been tree-ring dating or dendrochronology.

Most trees grow by adding yearly layers or rings of wood to their trunks, growing thicker rings in wet years and thinner rings in dry years and perhaps showing scars from fire damage. In a cross section

A vast library of tree ring patterns match and overlap back into time. Specimens taken from ruins, when matched and overlapped as indicated, progressively extend the tree ring dating back into prehistoric times.

Illustrations courtesy of the Laboratory of Tree-Ring Research, University of Arizona

CHAPTER 3: The Place

or core sample of the tree, the sequence of varying thicknesses in the rings forms a pattern reflecting the annual available moisture across a region. By matching the pattern of ring thickness in one tree to that of another from the same area but growing at a later (and overlapping) time period, a continuous record of tree ring patterns can be created from the oldest tree sample to the present day.

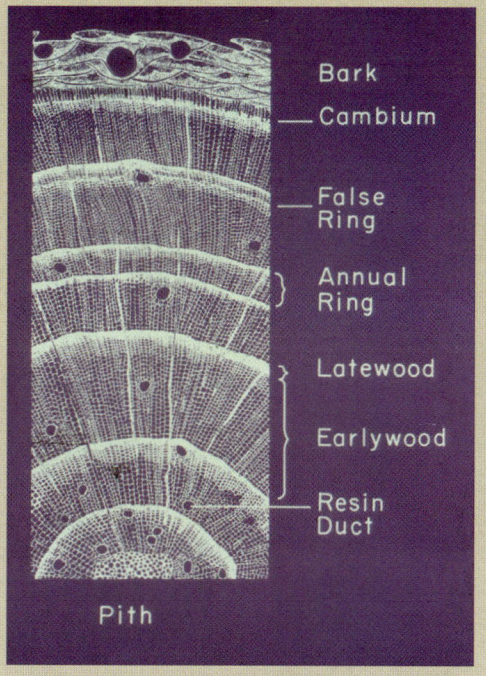

The pattern of a tree's rings tell of its place in history.

Illustrations courtesy of the Laboratory of Tree-Ring Research, University of Arizona

Using this library of unique ring patterns, a specimen of wood of unknown age can be compared to a known pattern. If a match is found, the age of the specimen can be assumed to be the same as the age of that part of the library pattern. The chance of two trees of very different ages having the exact same tree-ring pattern is fairly remote. This method, then, is considered quite reliable for determining the actual, rather than the relative age, of the sample.

When a tree is cut to build a structure, the outermost tree ring corresponds to the year the tree died and strongly suggests this was also the year, or close to it, when the building was constructed. The more wood samples and resulting pattern matches that can be made, the more reliable is the estimate of the age of the structure.

Visions of Chimney Rock

The pit house

Purists might call this an above-ground pit house; bedrock prevented deep excavation.

Photo by Helen L. Richardson

The next stage of evolution from the earliest jacal constructed houses was the pit house. The term pit house comes from the typical way these homes were constructed—partly or completely underground, surrounded by a wood or stone wall, and roofed by logs covered with adobe. However, the excavated pit house at Chimney Rock was built on the surface—on bedrock—and may also be called a surface pit house.

The fact that the pit house stands by itself convinced researcher Eddy that a nuclear family lived in it as well as in the other free-standing residences on the ridge. This nuclear-style family culture is in contrast to the more prevalent extended family culture of the Ancestral Puebloans.

In this excavated pit house, the circular living room is backed by three rectangular rooms. Artifacts found in the rooms suggest they were used for storage or as work rooms. The living room is walled by thick masonry made of local sandstone and laid in rough courses cemented with mud.

CHAPTER 3: The Place

Originally, the stone wall was reinforced by wooden posts and, during excavation, researchers found the interior lined with mud plaster covered with a white slip and displaying a few patches of red ochre paint. A secondary upper wall of poles and thatch reached to the roof. Entry was through a ladder placed through a hole in the roof.

When the source of heat is a fire in the middle of the house, air quality becomes an issue. The south wall of the pit house features an effective ventilator system composed of a vertical shaft and a horizontal tunnel. The inhabitants probably placed stone slabs in front of the shaft to keep air currents from blowing ashes and embers out of the fire pit. The fire pit was lined with clay and located slightly off center, perhaps so the entrance ladder could be propped in the smoke hole entryway.

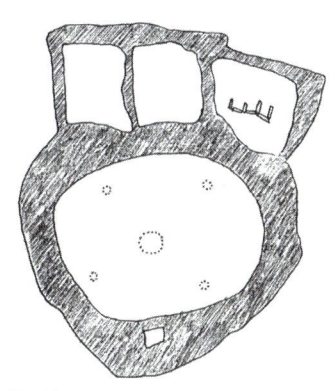

Pit House
Illustration from Chimney Rock Volunteer Handbook

Visitors to the Chimney Rock Archaeological Area view the partially reconstructed pit house as part of a volunteer-led tour.

Photo by Helen L. Richardson

Visions of Chimney Rock

This pit house used four upright roof support posts, three of which had clay plaster collars at their bases. These supports formed a square inside the walls of the pit house. The clay collars probably held the bottoms of the posts in place. Judging from the numerous impressions of poles in the fragments of burned clay, clay was also used to secure the cross-poles of the roof structure, and these supports display signs of orange pigment. After nearly a thousand years, the bright orange pieces still bear the finger marks of the builders.

When the pit house roof collapsed, it left enough burned logs and baked clay to allow archaeologists to reconstruct the roofing as a quadri-lateral frame covered by a flat roof and enclosed on the sides with leaners inclined from the main crossbeams to the top of the masonry wall.

The northern portion of the living room had four shallow holes filled with sand, which are thought to have served as rests for round-bottomed pottery vessels—possibly water jugs. The central room held several artifacts including a fourteen-quart corrugated jar. Researchers also found a cobble paint grinder that evidently was used to grind material for the red paint that decorated the walls. Several polishing stones, worn manos, axes, a whetstone, two lap anvils, and a small double-spouted, bifurcated gray jar were also found in this dwelling room.

The small rectangular rooms attached to the pit house were identified as workrooms based on the artifacts found in them. One room contained five or six stone-slab-lined bins for grinding or milling

The deep groove in the metate attests to the difficulty of grinding corn into meal.

Photo by John G. Richardson

CHAPTER 3: The Place

> **PRAYER PLUME HOLDERS**
>
> Four curious artifacts, interpreted as prayer plume holders, were found in the living room of the Pit House. Identical objects were described by Jeançon from his 1921 excavations of the Great House.
>
> These curved, sun-baked clay items, containing six holes poked into the clay, are similar to objects used in recent times.
>
> These artifacts provide a possible connection with the Chaco Canyon and Montezuma Basin cultures. Similar feather holders found at Pueblo Bonito in Chaco Canyon and at Wallace Ruin are made of the same type of clay as the Chimney Rock artifacts.
>
> *Based on present-day practices, these items are believed to be prayer plume holders used in ceremonies or rituals.*
> *Photo by John G. Richardson*

corn. Each bin probably held a flat sandstone slab with a curved basin (a metate) and a smaller hand-sized cobble or slab (the mano), which were used together to grind corn or beans or seeds. One metate was recovered during excavation, and the delicate stone slabs have been reconstructed. Originally this room was probably part of the round living room, since the clay floor extends under the dividing wall.

The middle room contained numerous hammer stones and several large choppers likely used for making stone tools. The choppers were made of hard, quartz-type, sharp-edged tool stone, and the hammer stones were hand-sized river cobbles with battered ends. Among the material found, a green cryptocrystalline quartz was traced to its source a few miles north along the Piedra River. This extremely hard rock sharpened well, enabling the toolmakers to craft knives and arrowheads.

Visions of Chimney Rock

The third room was evidently used for storage. A sub-floor cist contained charred maize and was topped with a wooden plank lid. Five large corrugated jars containing charred maize kernels, beans, and wild plant seeds were also excavated from this room. In addition to these plant foods, deer and elk bones indicated residents probably used this room for butchering meat.

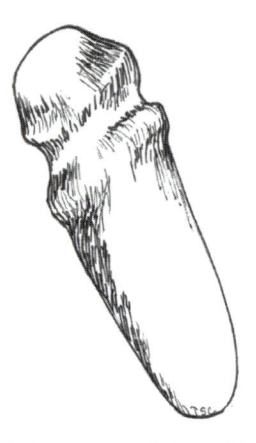

Using stone tools, it could take up to eight hours to cut and trim a 10-inch diameter tree.
Illustration by Jean Carson

This ax head is typical of tools used by the Ancestral Puebloans.

Photo by John G. Richardson

A plank lid found in this storage room was made from Douglas fir and ponderosa pine. Two inches thick, the plank was constructed in such a way that the grain ran lengthwise. Archaeologists theorize trees were split using hafted splitting axes, then planed with harder stone scrapers and choppers. Final smoothing probably called for softer sandstone abraders.

Beneath this pit house, stratigraphic evidence discloses an earlier circular sub-structure. Reflecting possible re-use of timbers, tree-ring dates from this site range from AD 872 to 1077. The largest number of wood samples contains at least a portion of the outer ring from the later date.

One reason for a range of dates is that, in addition to using fresh-cut timber, the builders also reused dead logs and timbers salvaged from

CHAPTER 3: The Place

older or abandoned structures. Cutting down a tree with a stone axe was a major operation so the pre-Puebloan people used whatever was at hand. Using stone implements, limited studies have shown it could take eight hours to cut a 10-inch diameter tree and trim it for use.

While tree-ring dating helps establish a timeline for construction of the structures at Chimney Rock, this piece of petrified wood found at the site is far older than any structure.

Photo by Helen L. Richardson

The youngest timber sample found—cut in AD 1077—showed incomplete outer growth rings, indicating it was logged during the growing season, probably between June and July. This pit house was quite probably built much earlier, but the existence of many pieces of wood from AD 1077 argues for extensive repairs during that year.

The Great Kiva

> ***"The kiva was the most distinctive structure in all the great centers of pre-historic life in North America, reaching the epitome of structural symbolism in the Great Kivas of the twelfth century."***
>
> Frank Waters, *The Book of the Hopi* (p. 127)

The Chimney Rock area boasts several small kivas, but the excavated and partially reconstructed Great Kiva remains an impressive structure. Modern use of kivas by the Pueblo people suggests such structures were used for both ritual and social activities.

Visions of Chimney Rock

Zuni Dancers feel privileged to dance at Chimney Rock as their ancestors might have danced centuries ago.

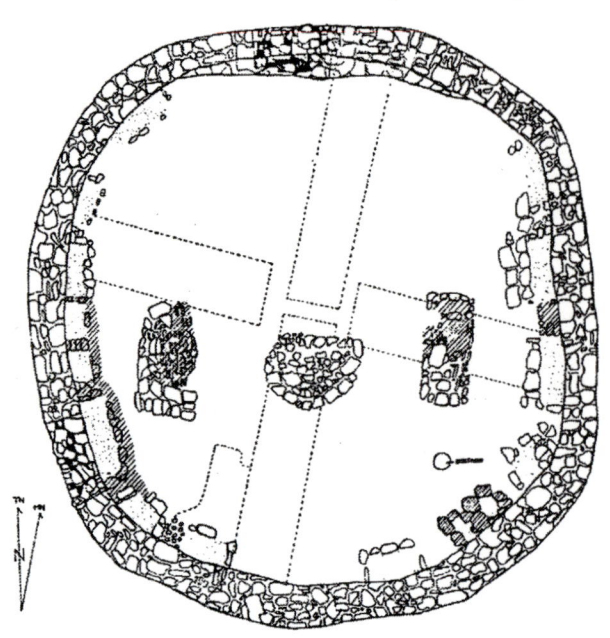

Photo used with permission of Fernando Cellicion

Great Kiva

Illustration from Chimney Rock Volunteer Handbook

CHAPTER 3: The Place

Great Kivas usually are larger and more elaborate than other kivas, although no two Great Kivas are exactly alike. While most are roughly circular, other shapes exist. At 41 to 44 feet across, the Great Kiva at Chimney Rock was likely designed to be large enough to hold women and children for community meetings and work as well as for religious ceremonies which may have been the domain of the community's men.

Kivas are normally underground structures, but Chimney Rock's heart of stone—the ubiquitous bedrock—prevented that. Built between approximately AD 994 and AD 1084, the Great Kiva lies in a village of nineteen masonry buildings located on the northwest rim of the lower mesa. The floor on the north side is directly on bedrock while the southern portion was filled in an attempt to make the floor somewhat level. The irregular, uneven courses of wall masonry showed no sign of being plastered.

An interior bench, sometimes called a banquette, was probably used for seating and placement of religious items. In some kivas, the bench is continuous; here it is only a short, irregular segment.

Excavators of the Great Kiva unearthed these artifacts now stored at the Anasazi Heritage Center in Dolores, CO.

Photo by John G. Richardson

A fire pit occupies a spot near the center of the floor. Although it was probably used for ceremonies, excavation revealed no signs of burning. Structures on either side of the fire pit are assumed to be walking drums or foot drums. While they are typical features of Great Kivas, archaeologists can only guess about their purpose. Burned wooden

Visions of Chimney Rock

planks were found in the foot drums in Chimney Rock's Great Kiva. Perhaps when danced upon, they produced a drumming rhythm.

Excavators unearthed fourteen sub-floor storage cists or vaults around the inside perimeter. Often present in kivas, nine of these sub-floor cists were covered with charred wooden lids. When excavating the cists, researchers also found a few small items—a stone ax, a bone awl, a piece of worked bone, a small mano, some pottery fragments, and burned clay.

Whether the Great Kiva ever had a roof has been a subject of much discussion with no conclusion. Although a ventilation shaft would have been necessary for an underground kiva, none was found in this structure. Great Kivas commonly had post holes which supported roofs of logs. In some Great Kivas, massive sandstone disks are found in the floor, supporting tree trunks that could have held up a heavy log and adobe roof (readily seen in the reconstructed Great Kiva at Aztec Ruins).

In Chimney Rock's Great Kiva, there are no such obvious remains. There is one small post hole in the floor, but no other signs of support posts have been found. While excavators

A cribbed roof on Chimney Rock's Great Kiva would have been a massive structure, similar to the roof on this replica Great Kiva at Aztec Ruins, Aztec, NM, and would have left considerable evidence of its existence.

Photo by Helen L. Richardson

CHAPTER 3: The Place

found ash, perhaps from a burned partial roof or sun shade, the sparse amount made it seem unlikely there would have been a solid, typically heavy kiva roof. As further evidence against a full roof, the kiva walls do not have doorways or openings, but are low enough to step over onto a bench or wooden ladder.

FATHER SUN

The kiva religion is a generic term to describe what probably was a variety of religions practiced by the kiva-building Ancestral Puebloans. Today, the Puebloans consider their traditional religions to be culture-specific and do not appreciate having them discussed or questioned by others.

Summer solstice sunrise is a spectacular sight from Chimney Rock's sun tower site, especially when the skies are smoky from summer wildfires. Photo by Helen L. Richardson

The late Dr. Alfonso Ortiz, a member of the San Juan Pueblo and an eminent anthropologist, wrote that the annual time clock of the sun was used to precisely time all of the activities and rituals of the pueblo. Each pueblo had its skywatchers to make certain all activities from cleaning irrigation ditches and building houses to rituals like blessing the corn and communal cleansing were accomplished on the date prescribed by that pueblo. Activities and rituals varied by pueblo as did the date.

"Father Sun was the most important and powerful of all the powers as it set all the times for all the rituals and activities," wrote Ortiz.

Visions of Chimney Rock

The stone basin site

The summer solstice sunrise lights up the modern-day fire tower as it rises above the Great House Pueblo, as seen from Chimney Rock's Stone Basin.
Photo by Helen L. Richardson

Near the Great Kiva, surrounded by a low circular wall of dry-laid stones, is a shallow, circular basin carved in the bedrock. While similar basins are found at Chaco Canyon and other Ancestral Puebloan sites across the region, no one knows for certain what their purpose may have been.

At typical Ancestral Puebloan sites, the basins are usually near a cliff that overlooks water. They also are close to other pueblos and agricultural areas and are usually within sight of a presumed shrine. Chimney Rock's stone basin is within view of the cliff overlooking the Piedra River and its fertile valley. From the site, you also can view the Great House, the Great Kiva, and the twin Chimney Rock pillars, which some believe may have been considered a shrine to the Ancestral Puebloans' twin warrior gods.

CHAPTER 3: The Place

SKYWATCHERS

Archeoastronomer Dr. J. McKim Malville found an interesting relationship between the position of Chimney Rock's stone basin and the summer solstice sunrise. On that day, someone standing at the stone basin will see the sun rise directly over the north wall of the Great House. This could have provided the inhabitants an important annual marker in their skywatching effort.

Three other marker sites are found in the upper mesa to mark the winter solstice and the two equinoxes. In each of these cases, the back sight is man-made and the fore sight is a natural rock formation. There is little doubt the solar observations were an essential part of the Ancestral Puebloan culture.

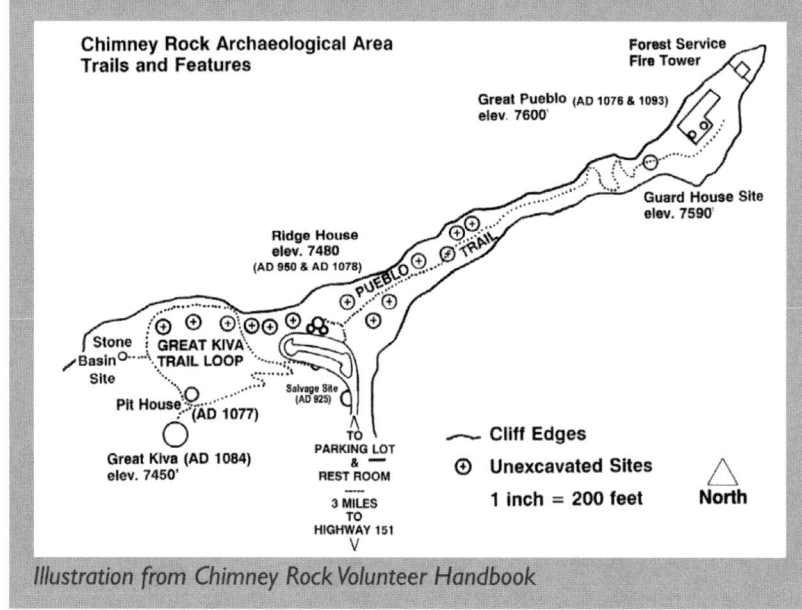

Illustration from Chimney Rock Volunteer Handbook

Unexcavated sites

Along the paved, wheelchair-accessible trail to the Great Kiva, visitors will see a number of mounds, sometimes with a shallow crater or depression in the top. These are the remains of pit houses or other structures abandoned to the elements by their builders. How did they come to be what we see today?

Visions of Chimney Rock

The typical pit house was built of thick stone walls cemented and plastered over with mud. The roof was built on a frame of logs, covered with smaller branches, brush, and slabs of stone or mud. When a pit house was abandoned or burned, the remains of the roof collapsed into the circular living room. The tops of the stone walls came down, forming a cone-shaped mound. The fallen debris of the upper walls protected the lower walls, and the roof remains protected the floor of the living room and whatever artifacts were inside.

Over the centuries, wind-blown sand and the remains of plants growing on the mound built up a thick cover, softening the mound and further protecting its secrets. When archaeologists excavate a pit house site, they must carefully peel away all the layers of covering and expose what was protected beneath the debris.

What is hidden in these undisturbed sites? Perhaps little more than burned wood and broken ceramics...but until excavation, the secrets remain hidden.

Salvage site

The secrets of the Salvage Site have been all but lost in the modern day balancing act between providing access for people to see and learn and sacrificing part of a people's history. Before portions of the site were lost to road construction and parking lot expansion, it was partially excavated. Researchers found the site to have been a multi-room, masonry-walled building containing two large circular rooms, a large number of small round rooms, and a ramada on the northwest corner. The multiple large rooms suggest the residents practiced an extended family culture.

At the salvage site, the masonry walls went all the way to the roof and supported it. Even though wood dated the building to AD 925—making it 152 years older than the excavated Pit House and the oldest structure excavated in the Chimney Rock Archaeological Area—there were no jacal (stick and mud) walls. Yet the excavation revealed two prayer plume holders similar to those found at the Pit House.

CHAPTER 3: The Place

Salvage Site

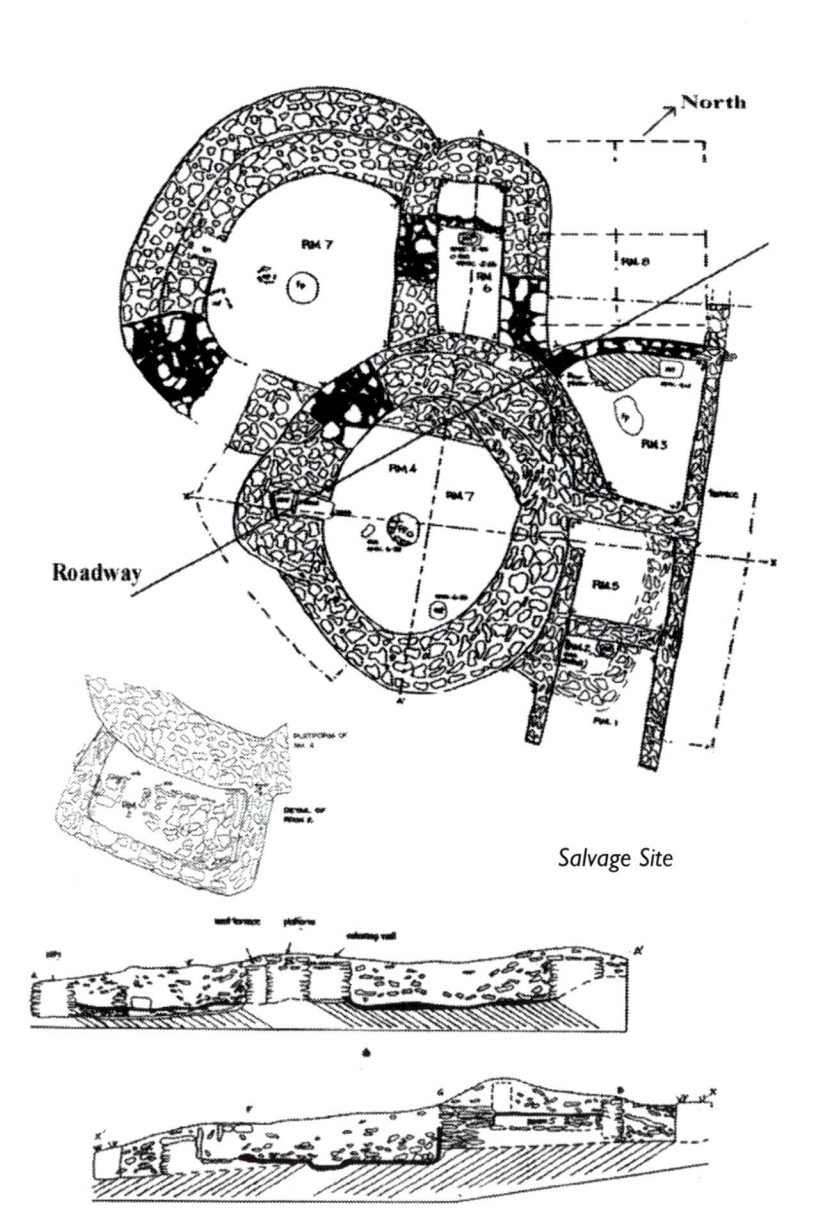

Illustration from Chimney Rock Volunteer Handbook

Visions of Chimney Rock

The Ridge House

At somewhat higher elevation than the Pit House and Great Kiva, a complex of structures known as the Ridge House is made up of three circular residences with a block of two rectangular work rooms attached. Dendrochronology indicates one residence was constructed and occupied about AD 950 and may have been built over an even older structure. The two other residences were added about AD 1078 and were likely two stories high.

The Ridge House was last occupied approximately AD 1125. Tree-ring dating and the pottery sherds found in the rooms show the time frame to be Pueblo II, which is dated between AD 925 and 1125. The presence of a few pieces of exotic Tusayan black-on-red trade ware, dated between AD 1050 and the 1200s, strongly suggests the residents were late Pueblo II period.

One of the oldest pieces of wood, dated AD 883, was found as the lintel to the ventilator tunnel in the center room. Other wood, dating from AD

Ridge House

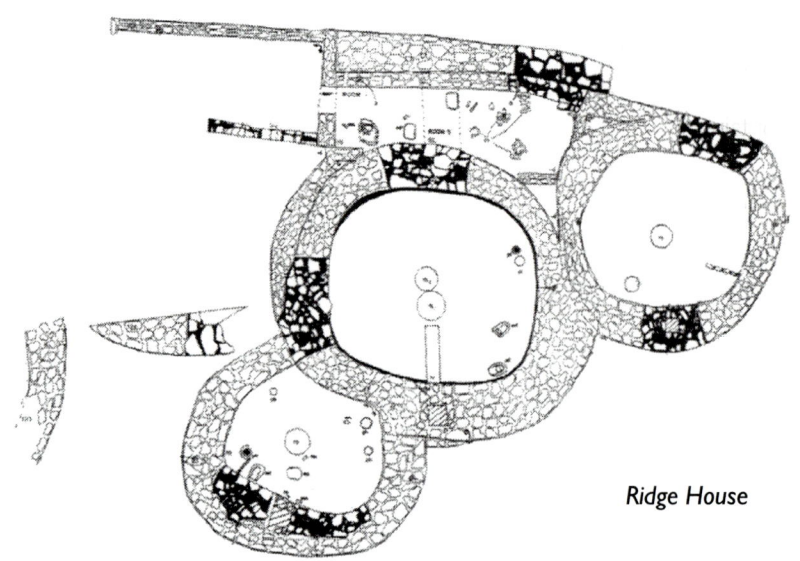

Illustration from Chimney Rock Volunteer Handbook

CHAPTER 3: The Place

1072 and AD 1078, indicate additions or repairs at these times. An earlier structure under the work and storage area was intentionally filled with trash and with wood dating no later than AD 1056. Since it was common to reuse older material or downed trees, these dates are a reasonable indication of the time frame of use.

The Ridge House most likely housed an extended family.
Photo by L. Larason for the US Forest Service

Canteen sherd
Photo by John G. Richardson

Architecturally, the three residences of the Ridge House were more like the Salvage Site residence than the Pit House in that the masonry walls went all the way to and supported the roof. The walls were thick and made with uneven courses of large stones, then plastered with mud. Each room had a ventilator shaft and fire pit, metates and manos for milling corn, and two rooms contained post holes for a roof or possibly ladder sockets.

Interestingly, the Ridge House's three pit houses shared the same work and storage space, indicating to anthropologists it might have been occupied by an extended family.

Sites along the Great House trail yielded artifacts now housed in the Anasazi Heritage Center in Dolores, CO.

Photos by John G. Richardson

Visions of Chimney Rock

Pueblo trail pit houses

As modern-day visitors hike up the Great Pueblo trail from the Ridge House, they can see numerous unexcavated ruins—some partly exposed and some still completely buried—lining the causeway to the upper mesa. These may be pit houses similar to the excavated Pit House site on the lower trail. Along the narrow spine of rock leading up to the Great House Pueblo, some of these pit houses were built separately, some in clusters. Of the ten mounds found along this trail, two were excavated but were neither back-filled nor reconstructed. While some original masonry is visible in the walls of two sites, their unprotected state has allowed considerable deterioration to occur.

These potsherds were found near the top of the Pueblo Trail.
Photo courtesy of the Anasazi Heritage Center

The minimal excavation that was performed at these sites revealed artifacts such as potsherds, metates, a mano, an axe head, a bone awl, and a prayer feather holder. A storage bin containing a little charred corn also was found in one of the rooms.

The first excavation was done by the original archaeological expedition led by Jeançon and Roberts in the early 1920s. At that time, Jeançon also found evidence of paving on the north side of one of the pit houses. He uncovered thin slabs of sandstone filled between with very hard plaster. Even though there are no other indications of a Chacoan road to Chimney Rock, some researchers theorize this might be a remnant of a Chacoan road.

Another curious find at the pueblo trail site speaks to the creativity of the Ancestral Puebloans. On the northwest corner of one room, a

CHAPTER 3: The Place

Since storms tended to bypass Chimney Rock's mesa top, capturing what little moisture did fall required ingenuity.
  Photo by Helen L. Richardson

portion of the wall protruded to the outside. On top of this was a slab of sandstone with a circular depression and a groove leading to the edge of the sandstone. This was placed, Jeançon surmised, so a pot could be set under it to catch water running down the groove. This catchment system could have been a very practical answer to the lack of water on Chimney Rock, and it's an indication of the effort needed to acquire and preserve the precious element.

The Guardhouse site

Whether to preserve the peace or welcome visitors to the Great House Pueblo, at the top of the rough stone stairway on the lower end of the Chimney Rock mesa are remnants of a nearly vanished building now called the Guardhouse. Little remains today, but this structure may have controlled traffic to the Great House since it commands the only entrance from the narrow causeway to the large structure built atop the mesa.

Early excavators found the Guard House consisted of a single circular room surrounded by a rectangular wall. The room is directly on the bedrock while the terracing within the rectangular area was built up two to three feet in height—whether to level the floor or to provide a commanding view is conjecture. The walls of the building were well constructed of fine small stones. In the center of the very hard floor of

Visions of Chimney Rock

Guardhouse

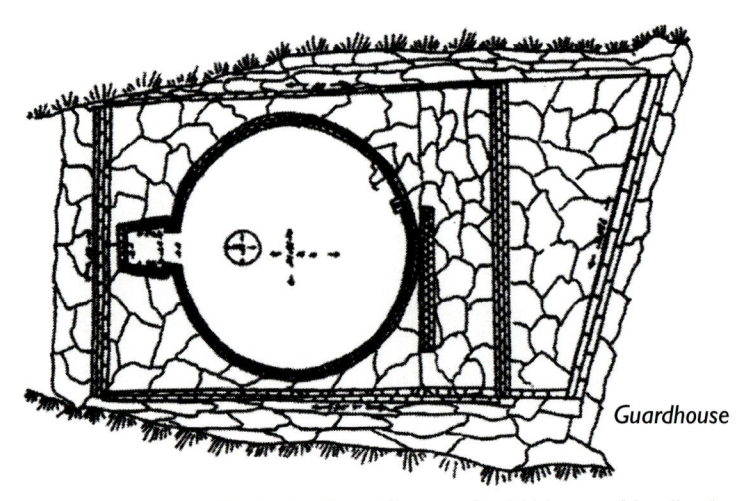

Illustration from Chimney Rock Volunteer Handbook

one inch thick adobe was a large fireplace completely filled with ashes. Near this fireplace, a storage place was set into the floor. Recessed into the wall next to this storage place was a small, well-made cupboard built of small stones. It contained a circular depression with a raised margin forming a good pot rest.

On the western side of the circle, a small room extended toward the outer wall. Items found near the entrance to this room included a fine bear fetish made of clay, an axe head, a chisel made from an antler, a pigment grinder, bone awls, fragments of a large decorated bowl, and remains of a charred basket.

The Guard House site offers a commanding view of the narrow trail to the Great House.

Photo by Scott Allen, Mountain Snapshot

64

CHAPTER 3: The Place

Charred corn was found mingled with the charred roof material on the floor of the structure. A paved lintel more than a foot deep was fitted above a doorway.

Jeançon concluded the purpose of the Guard House was not ceremonial because so much of the material found indicated secular use. In spite of the site's name, there also seems to be little evidence of its use as a defensive position to protect the Great House Pueblo. Perhaps instead of defending the Great House, the site was more like a welcome center.

Behold the Great House

Both by its location and by its architecture, the Great House on the mesa top is the most dramatic building so far examined at Chimney Rock, and yet the most mysterious. Great Houses in the Four Corners area generally were built with more or less standardized Chacoan architecture and masonry styles. At the height of Chacoan cultural development—about AD 900 to 1150—a Great House consisted of a large, well-planned pueblo building with multiple stories, large rooms, and subterranean ceremonial chambers known as great kivas. Great Houses were associated with a village or community of farmers, artisans, and other folk who, perhaps, provided labor, supplies, and food for the Chacoans. This complex of pueblo and community, when located at a distance from Chaco Canyon, is known as an "outlier."

Even though Chimney Rock was officially declared a Chacoan outlier by the US Congress in 1995, its relationship with Chaco is questionable to some who have studied the site. Many scholars believe the Great Houses were devised and administered by a Chacoan elite who supplied resources from the outliers to Chaco Canyon in New Mexico, center of the culture. Other outliers include Aztec and Salmon Ruins in New Mexico and the Escalante Ruin and Yucca House in Colorado.

In fact, the nature of Chacoan influence at Chimney Rock is being challenged. On a case-by-case basis, some investigators require finding

Visions of Chimney Rock

The Great House Pueblo perches on the very top of the mesa, at the feet of the twin pinnacles.
Photo courtesy of the US Forest Service, Pagosa District

Chacoan elite artifacts at an outlier before accepting the theory of Chacoan occupation. Others consider architecture of elements such as a Great House and Great Kiva, ceramics, and contemporaneity to determine association. Chimney Rock may not have been Chacoan occupied, but it was definitely Chacoan influenced.

CHAPTER 3: The Place

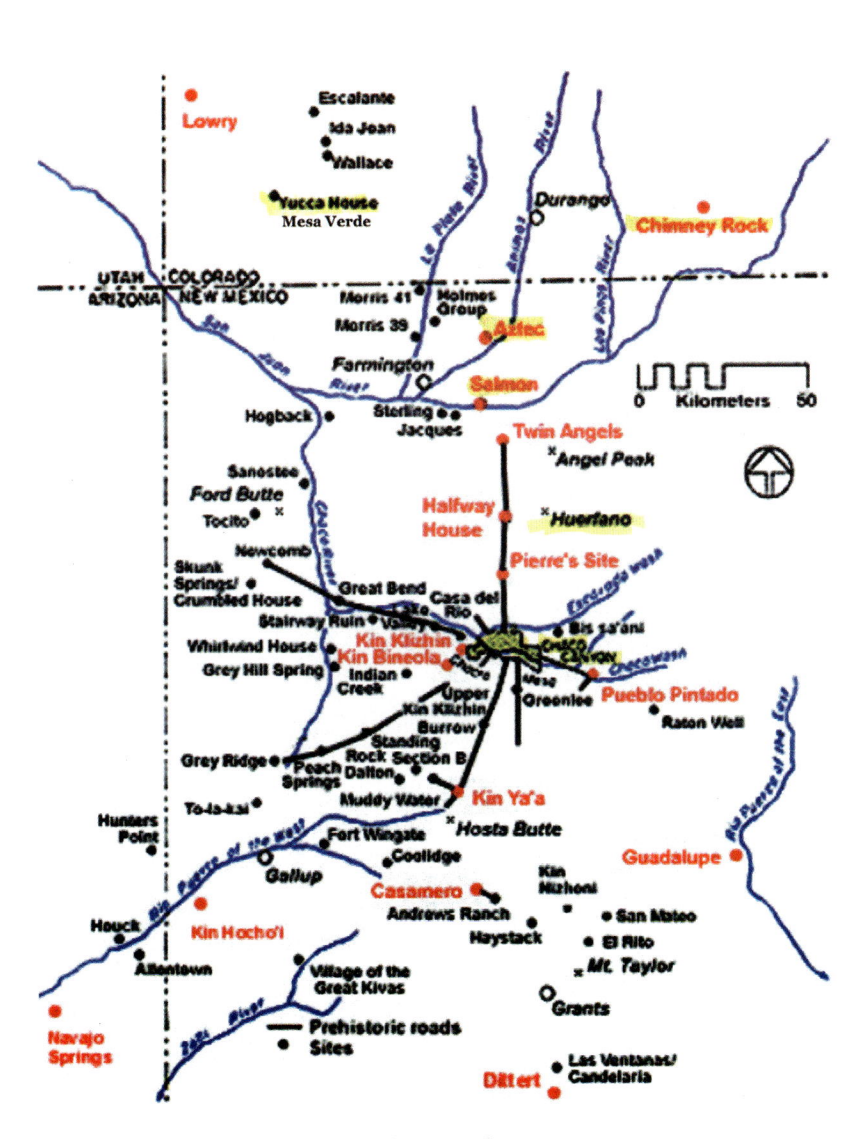

Chimney Rock's relationship to the Chacoan Community.
Illustration from Chimney Rock Volunteer Handbook

Visions of Chimney Rock

Regardless of the affiliation with Chaco, it has been demonstrated that signal fires from Huerfano Mesa—visible sixty-five miles to the south of Chimney Rock—could be seen both at Chimney Rock and Chaco Canyon, allowing long-distance communication between the two communities.

Chacoan influence

If the Chacoan elite did not build the Great House, who did? One theory suggests Chacoan construction specialists may have been borrowed to supervise the construction by local people. This theory supposes the local people wanted to build a Great House after seeing one in Chaco or elsewhere. This theory makes it unnecessary to find Chaco elite artifacts at Chimney Rock.

Another theory has to do with the purpose of the Chacoan Great House. It supposes the Chacoan influence over Ancestral Puebloan outliers was instigated and held together by getting the citizens of outliers to

The Chimney Rock Great House may have been a gathering place for the seven communities surrounding Chimney Rock.

Photo by Scott Allen, Mountain Snapshots

CHAPTER 3: The Place

travel to Chaco (perhaps a pilgrimage in today's terms) and stay in the Great Houses where social and religious ceremonies would unite them. The presence of a Great House defines Chimney Rock as a Chacoan outlier.

Chacoan Great Houses may have been ancient motels where pilgrims from afar gathered for social or religious purposes.

Photo by Helen L. Richardson

In the case of the Chimney Rock Great House, the several local communities may have been held together by similar pilgrimages where goods were exchanged, social and religious ceremonies shared, and general bonding occurred.

The influence of Chaco's culture was clearly established at Chimney Rock by AD 1076 and continued through at least AD 1093. This timeline is indicated by tree ring dating of the logs used to build the Great House.

Assuming Chacoan influence, the location and characteristics of the Great House allow archaeologists to guess at its purpose. The position suggests one of its main uses was to observe the twin pinnacles. The long

Visions of Chimney Rock

axis of the building aims directly at the two spires, but this could merely reflect the best use of the long, narrow mesa top. It is also probable Chimney Rock and Companion Rock represent a shrine to the Ancestral Puebloans' twin warrior gods or other deities.

Is it merely coincidence that the main axis of Chimney Rock's Chacoan Great House leads the eye to the rock towers?
Photo courtesy of the US Forest Service, Pagosa District

Archaeoastronomers believe the location was selected as a solar and lunar observatory. In particular, they suggest the site is ideal for watching the phenomenon known as the major lunar standstill, an 18.6-year cycle of the moon. At the peak of the cycle, the moon rises between the stone pillars as seen from the Great House.

Another theory supposes the local people of Chimney Rock built the Great House, imitating the architectural style of Chaco Canyon. This theory needs the support of another theory—that the Chacoan Great Houses, whether in Chaco Canyon or located in an outlier, were used as pilgrimage destinations for people buying into the Chaco phenomenon, possibly for spiritual or economic reasons.

CHAPTER 3: The Place

The photo below shows how the smaller shaped stones used as chinking in the Great House Pueblo at Chimney Rock mimic those at Pueblo Bonito in Chaco Canyon, pictured on the right.
Photos by Dick Moseley

On the other hand, the Chimney Rock Great House may also have been used to entice surrounding Chimney Rock communities to make local pilgrimages to the Great House for unification. The large number of metates found in the Great House seems to echo the similar overabundance of metates at Chaco Canyon's Pueblo Bonito, thought to have been supplied to pilgrimage visitors for preparing their food.

Another possible explanation for the placement of the Chimney Rock Great House is defense. High points of land are easily defended, and the limited access to the mesa would fit that need. The abundance of wild plants and animals in the surrounding forest may have been attractive to people from outside the region, such as the ancestors of today's Ute Indians. Jeançon and Roberts recognized the defensive potential of the site, but theorized that perhaps strife between groups of the Ancestral

Visions of Chimney Rock

Puebloan people themselves made defense necessary. More recent work casts doubt on the defensive nature of the structures.

Another theory is that raids by other Ancestral Puebloan groups against the Chimney Rock people forced the defensive construction of a stone-walled fortress on high ground to protect the people and their precious storerooms of food. However, there is no factual evidence yet found of violence nor of accumulated defensive weaponry at the Great House to support this theory. Since the only reliable source of water was the river 1,000 feet below the mesa top, this was a poor defensive site.

Perhaps the narrow, nearly inaccessible mesa helped protect ancient inhabitants from enemy attacks.
Photo courtesy of the US Forest Service, Pagosa District

Great House Pueblo
Illustration from Chimney Rock Volunteer Handbook

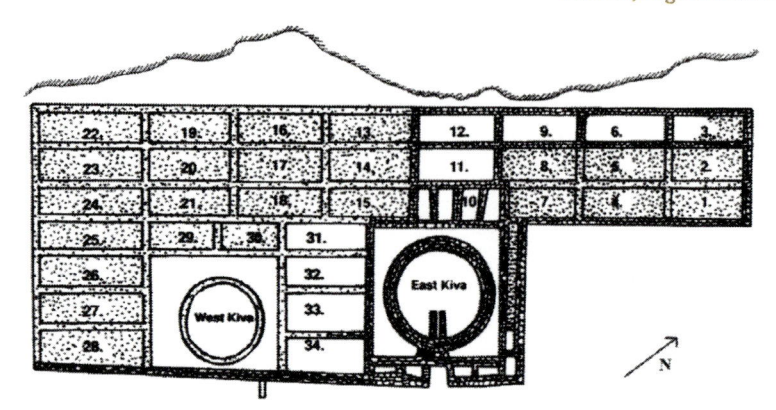

CHAPTER 3: The Place

Construction techniques

According to Jeançon, "Originally the building must have presented an imposing picture as it rose above the caprock to a height of not less than twenty feet and perhaps more."

The Great House Pueblo was L-shaped, two hundred and nine feet on the longest side and seventy feet at the widest point. About thirty-five rooms made up the ground floor while parts of the pueblo likely were two stories high.

In its prime, the Great House Pueblo most likely rose twenty feet above the top of the mesa.
Historic photo courtesy of the US Forest Service, Pagosa District

The distinctive Chacoan-style architecture of the Great House Pueblo displays finished surface stones laid in even courses, with small chips or chinking stones laid between and around larger stones. Inner and outer veneers of this masonry sandwich a core of rubble and earth to form thick

73

Visions of Chimney Rock

The Chacoan-style masonry of the Great House Pueblo (left) is much more complex than the stone courses of the Great Kiva (below).

Photos courtesy of the US Forest Service

and finely laid walls. The beautiful stonework visible today was not the final product. A finishing layer of mud plaster completely covered the walls.

The Great House Pueblo was a massive construction job "that was, in part at least, built on a pre-conceived plan," according to Jeançon, "evidenced by certain of the long walls which are continuous and with the partition walls put in afterwards."

Estimating from known construction methods and the results of Jeançon's and Roberts' excavations in 1921, the pueblo was built of some six million individual stones, 25,000 tons of earth and clay, and 5,000 logs. If you add the amount of water needed to mix the mud mortar and plaster as well as the food, water, and firewood required to supply the workers, occupants, and users of the site every day, you'll see it was an amazing accomplishment for this physically small community.

CHAPTER 3: The Place

The twin kivas

The east kiva is one of two that dominate the large structure at the top of the mesa.

Photo by Dick Moseley

Most rooms in the pueblo are rectangular, but there are two circular rooms, probably kivas. These rooms share features of known kivas at Chaco Canyon and may have served a similar purpose at Chimney Rock.

Both kivas share a common exterior wall (the south wall), which encloses the pueblo structure. Along the Pueblo Trail, visitors may see up close the quality of the Chacoan-style masonry and contrast it with the masonry style of the pit houses and Great Kiva farther down the mesa.

The south wall contains both reconstructed masonry and original stonework. The dark brown courses of stone in the lowest few feet of the wall are original. This long wall is part of what may be a buttress

Visions of Chimney Rock

system supporting the inner walls against the weight of the earth fill surrounding the round kivas inside their square walls.

A volunteer tour guide points out the original masonry in the Great House.

Photo by Helen L. Richardson

A lower wall was constructed along the outside wall of the east kiva facing Chimney Rock. This may have been another supporting buttress wall, but it also could have served as a bench from which the rocks could be seen. Today the view is obscured by the modern fire lookout tower and a stand of oak brush.

A volunteer-led tour ponders the location of rooms and kivas in Chimney Rock's partially excavated and restored Great House Pueblo.

Photo by Helen L. Richardson

CHAPTER 3: The Place

> **SYMMETRY AND ASYMMETRY**
> The distinctive division of the Great House places the residences rather equally on the east and west sides of the building—coincidence or purposefully symmetrical? In Chacoan cultures, this type of symmetry suggests the equality of dual governments or moieties. Another distinctive division of the Great House places the kivas and plazas on the south and the residences on the north. This asymmetrical division may suggest the contrast between the sacred and the non-sacred.

The east kiva, the larger of the two, is an above-ground kiva surrounded by dirt fill between the exterior wall of the kiva and a square enclosure wall. The inner wall of the kiva is lined by a five-foot high banquette, which may have been used to hold ceremonial items.

In the east kiva, roof beams rested upon horizontal logs placed in the notches located at intervals along the banquette. Jeançon and Roberts, who excavated the structure in 1921, were perplexed by the roof structure. The roof was burned so they could only guess at its construction. Eddy, who reexcavated the site in 1970-1972, felt the roof

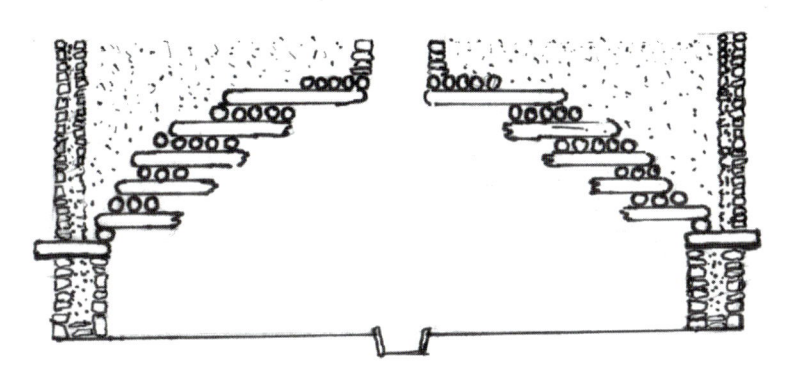

Cribbed roofs required massive amounts of time and timber.

Illustration by Jean Carson

structure was likely to be the Chaco-style cribbed-roof method which allowed ample headroom (examples can be seen at Aztec Ruins, New Mexico, and Mesa Verde National Park, Colorado).

The low bench may have been used for sitting or to hold items for ceremonies.
Photo courtesy of the US Forest Service, Pagosa District

The east kiva has the typical kiva features of fire box and ventilator tunnel, air shaft and keyhole (the recessed part of the wall containing the air shaft). The rectangular firebox is unusual—they're typically round—and it was placed off-center rather than in line with the air shaft. Three storage boxes, which were oriented generally to the cardinal directions (north, south, east, and west), were found set into the floor along with the well-defined fire box. Jeançon believed that the storage boxes took the place of wall niches, since none were found in the walls of the kiva. There are no signs of a deflector nor were there any pilasters present. The circular form, banquette, and ventilators are the items suggesting a kiva.

Eddy's findings on tree-ring dating validated the stratigraphic order of construction of the east kiva, with the first floor built in AD 1076 and the second construction or repair seventeen years later in AD 1093. These dates coincide with the occurance of major northern lunar standstills, reinforcing the theory that the Chimney Rock site was an important lunar and solar observatory.

Unlike the larger, more elaborate east kiva, the west kiva has no keyhole nor roof-beam notches on its banquette. It does have a surrounding fill of earth

CHAPTER 3: The Place

This historic photo shows reconstruction of the Great House, well under way.
Photo courtesy of the US Forest Service, Pagosa District

within an enclosing wall, and the step-like construction against the outer face of the southern enclosing wall may be a supporting buttress. No tree-ring evidence has been found to determine when the west kiva was built.

Visions of Chimney Rock

THE FIRE LOOKOUT TOWER

The stone-based fire lookout tower on the Chimney Rock mesa top was built in 1939 by the Civilian Conservation Corps and served as a working fire lookout until the late 1950s. The location was not ideal since the rock towers blocked the view to the northeast and the lookout ranger had to walk a long and dangerous trail past the rocks to check for the tell-tale column of smoke that signaled a wildfire.

The reconstructed fire tower affords a spectacular view of Chimney Rock and Companion Rock.

Photo by Mark Roper, US Forest Service

When a new tower was added at Devil Mountain to the west, it took over the job. The Chimney Rock tower was closed and abandoned in 1956. The deck and cabin of the original tower became weakened and unsafe and were torn down in 1966, leaving only the stone base.

In 1987, as part of the recreational development of the site, the tower's deck and cabin were rebuilt on the original stone base. This restoration allows you to see what fire towers looked like before helicopters and other modern means were used to spot fires in the National Forest. The "fire finder" in the center of the tower was used to determine the direction and distance to fires and was the original equipment for this tower.

CHAPTER 3: The Place

Room 8

In 1921, several rooms of the Great House Pueblo were left unexcavated. The room identified today as Room 8 was carefully excavated in 1970-1972 by Eddy and is open to view. The walls of this room exhibit a masonry style like that of Pueblo Bonito in Chaco Canyon—faced masonry construction and chinking which "indicates the prehistoric masons were trained in the tradition of Chaco Canyon," notes Eddy.

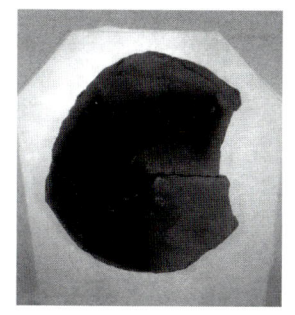

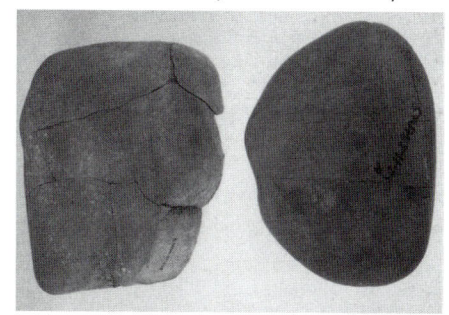

These ancient artifacts were found during excavation of Room 8 in the Great House Pueblo.

Photos courtesy of the Anasazi Heritage Center

When cleared, the walls of Room 8 stood as high as six feet nine inches along the east side. Remaining walls indicate a second story existed. A hatchway door, located in the northwest corner of the room, offered ladder access to a room above. Several pots and burned baskets were found in the debris-filled room.

The position of the artifacts from Room 8 further suggest a concern for traffic patterns. The heat and light for the room were from a fire built in an informally prepared, basin-shaped pit set off center so as to be out of alignment with the doorway. Movable containers for food storage, food service,

A scarcity of debris in Room 8 of the Great House Pueblo may indicate occasional long-term use or intensive use of short duration.

Photo courtesy of the Anasazi Heritage Center

Visions of Chimney Rock

and food preparation were provided by two coiled baskets and seven pottery vessels placed near the walls in all quarters of the room except the northwest quadrant. A large number of potsherds found in this room represent locally made black-on-white decorated, corrugated, plain gray, and trade pottery. The local black-on-white decorated ware included several pieces of Mancos and Wetherill black-on-white of Pueblo II age. Some San Juan White Ware, Mesa Verde Corrugated, and Payan Corrugated were found, but very few Pueblo I and no Pueblo III ceramics. These pottery styles strongly indicate occupation from about AD 1094 (Pueblo II period).

These dates are supported by tree-ring dating. Many examples of wood in the roof fall show several logs were cut during the summer of AD 1093 with none from earlier dates to indicate salvage from prior structures and none from later dates, meaning the roof stayed in good condition until it was destroyed by fire.

Archaeoastronomy

The importance of astronomy to early agricultural societies is widely accepted by researchers in the field. Skywatchers would affirm that the rhythms of life and time were on schedule and doing well. Planting and harvest, ceremonies, and the happenings in the sky would synchronize with life itself.

Archaeologists who have studied the Chimney Rock area disagree on whether there is special meaning in the two stone

Experts speculate the mesa beneath the twin pinnacles might have been a solar or lunar observatory. This preview of a lunar standstill moonrise in March 2004 catches the moon emerging from behind Chimney Rock.

Photo by Helen L. Richardson

CHAPTER 3: The Place

pinnacles for the people who built their structures beneath their shadow, possibly as solar or lunar observatories. The controversy over the importance of archaeo-astronomy—the branch of science that studies how these ancient cultures related to and predicted the movements of the heavenly bodies—likely will continue as long as the twin pinnacles are visible.

From Peterson Mesa across the Piedra River, skywatchers likely tracked the sunrise between the stone pinnacles on the spring and fall equinoxes.
Photo courtesy of the US Forest Service,

We can assume the Ancestral Puebloans who lived at Chimney Rock, like their counterparts throughout the southwest, were keen observers of the sky. In the second half of the Eleventh Century, there was much to see. It was a period of many strange and wonderful events which would have been noticed and marveled at by these people. Imagine seeing the supernova of July 4, 1054 which created the Crab Nebula, a newly-formed star visible even in the daytime and casting a strong shadow by night. These people also witnessed Halley's Comet in AD 1066, a total solar eclipse near Chaco Canyon in AD 1076, another at Chimney Rock in AD 1097, and a period of intense

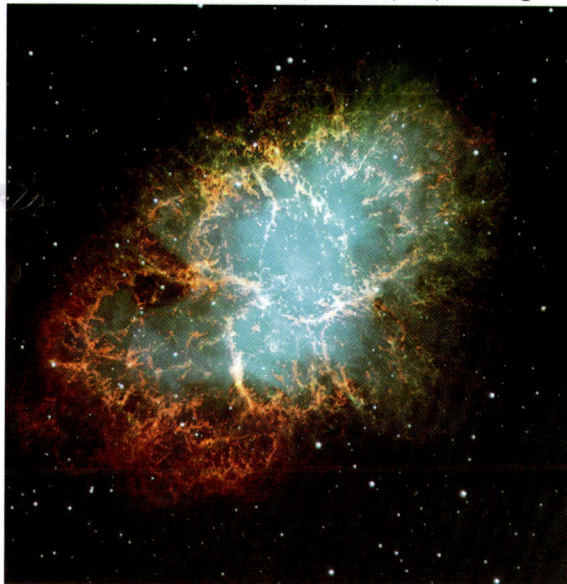

Crab Nebula
Photo from the Southern European Observatory Website

83

Visions of Chimney Rock

sunspots in AD 1077, in addition to the usual comings and goings of the planets, stars, sun, and moon.

At Chimney Rock, all four quarters of the year are marked by man-made features using natural or man-made foresight. A stone tower near the present-day parking lot likely was a solar observatory marking the winter solstice sunrises over the east slope. From the stone basin, the Ancestral Puebloans could watch the sun rise over the north wall of the Great House on the summer solstice. Across the Piedra River on Peterson Mesa, a structure in the Chacoan architectural style could have been a vantage point for watching the sun rise between Chimney Rock and Companion Rock on both the spring and fall equinoxes.

Whether coincidence or planned, the Great House Pueblo is a natural observatory for another astronomical event—the major lunar standstill. The moon's orbit of Earth oscillates or wobbles, gradually causing the moon to rise at different points on the horizon over the years. The entire cycle of wobbling north to south and north again takes 18.6 years to complete. At each end of its swing, the moon pauses for about three years, rising at the same point on the horizon before beginning to move back toward the opposite end of the swing. This pause is known as a major lunar standstill.

In 1988, Dr. J. McKim Malville and his team of graduate students captured this time-lapse photo, the first image of the moon rising between Chimney Rock and Companion Rock, as viewed from the Great House, during a major lunar standstill.

Photo courtesy of Dr. J. McKim Malville

CHAPTER 3: The Place

In 1987, Dr. J. McKim Malville, an astronomer at the University of Colorado at Boulder, predicted and then demonstrated that, at its northern standstill, the moon would rise between Chimney Rock and Companion Rock at the winter solstice as viewed from the Great House.

MAJOR LUNAR STANDSTILL

The moon, like the sun, rises at different places on the horizon throughout the year. Careful observation will demonstrate that these times and places of moonrise recur at regular, predictable intervals. The interval between full moonrises we call a month. The moon also moves to a longer cycle, lasting 18.6 years. This grand sweep travels the eastern horizon from south to north every month. The most northerly of these monthly moonrises are the ones that allow the 18.6 year standstill cycle to be perceived by naked eye astronomers.

At sunset near the winter solstice, the glow signals the moon's arrival in the gap between Chimney Rock's stone pillars.
Photo by Helen L. Richardson

The majestic natural stone pillars of Chimney Rock have a unique connection to the major standstill of the moon. Seen from the Great House, the stone towers are slightly out of line with each other, framing a narrow window of sky between them. At sunset near the day of the

Visions of Chimney Rock

winter solstice during the major lunar standstill, the full moon rises exactly between the stone pillars, caught in this thin window of sky, and is visible only from this one vantage point high on the narrow mesa.

Malville suggested this phenomenon could have been the reason for the construction of Chimney Rock's Chacoan-style Great House. Certainly, anyone who was on the Chimney Rock mesa during the lunar standstill could not have missed the moonrise between those stone pillars. Lunar standstills occurred in AD 1056-1057, 1075-1076, 1094-1095, and 1112-1113. Tree-ring dates place the periods of major construction of the Great House Pueblo at AD 1076 and 1093—the former concurring with a lunar standstill and the latter perhaps anticipating the next lunar standstill cycle.

In AD 1076, when the Great House was built, the moon was rising between the rock towers. In AD 1093-94, when the Great House

From the stone basin, the lunar standstill moon rises to the north of the twin pinnacles.

Photo by John G. Richardson

CHAPTER 3: The Place

was expanded, the moon was again rising between the rock towers. This may be nothing more than coincidence. However, researchers in archaeoastronomy see more possibilities. Malville proposes that Chimney Rock's people were more than just aware of these events. He suggests they celebrated them, in part by constructing the Great House to mark and revere the beautiful and rare lunar events captured or protected by Chimney Rock's twin monoliths.

The alignment between the Great House and the Chimney Rock pillars and the moon is real. It has been calculated, surveyed, and confirmed. The question that remains unanswered is its cultural and spiritual importance to the Ancestral Puebloans of Chimney Rock. Despite the impressive record of archaeological research, we face a mystery that may never be solved. Was the lunar standstill an event of spiritual awe and wonder to them, or just another pretty but meaningless happening in the sky?

Even without written records, the Chacoan builders left clues in the very fabric of the Chimney Rock Great House. The Great House is located on the closest patch of ground to the twin pillars, on the highest level area above the valley floor 1,000 feet below. The difficulty of carrying stone and tree trunks and earth and water up the narrow path and keeping its people fed and warm and supplied with water argues powerfully that this was an important place to be.

The question of how they built this impressive structure may provide the most intriguing information of all. Many Chacoan pueblos are aligned along a north/south axis. This is not so at Chimney Rock. Architecturally, the long walls of the building are not parallel. The northerly long wall lines up with a small basin carved in solid bedrock 2,000 feet southwest of and below the Great House. If you stand at the stone basin and look at the northerly wall of the Great House at the time of summer solstice, you will see that the sun rises centered on this wall. Viewed from this same stone basin, the southerly point on the Great House lines up to a spot in the sky where the Crab Nebula Supernova appeared for three weeks around July 4 in the year AD 1054.

In addition to its alignments with the Crab Nebula Supernova and the summer solstice sunrise, the Great House Pueblo connects the narrow

Visions of Chimney Rock

gap between the rock spires with the rising moon during the major lunar standstill. It stands at the only spot where the moonrise can be seen at the peak of the 18.61-year cycle.

By themselves, these facts can't prove the Great House was specifically constructed to celebrate the sun or stars or the lunar standstill. But they do imply that the people of Chimney Rock were skywatchers. They observed, they remembered, and they may have captured sky cycles and events by linking their buildings to them through natural features and architectural alignments.

When the moon reaches its northernmost point every 18.6 years, skywatchers at the Great House Pueblo could observe the full moon's rise between the rock pinnacles in the dead of winter, as it did on December 26, 2004.

Photo by Helen L. Richardson

If Chimney Rock mesa was the center of a place dedicated to the watching of the moon, there were also sites and places nearby that saw other celestial events and cycles. The view from a small structure along the eastern cliff edge below the twin spires, today known as the Sun

CHAPTER 3: The Place

Tower, provides a day-to-day solar calendar as the sun rises over the sharp mountain peaks and valleys of the eastern horizon. Across the Piedra River to the west, the high, long cliff of Peterson Ridge affords an eastward view that captures the two Chimney Rock towers in profile as the sun rises between them. From north to south along the cliff, the first rays of the rising sun fall on a series of buildings and mark the days from late January through the Summer Solstice in June to the Winter Solstice in December, before beginning the return trip to the north.

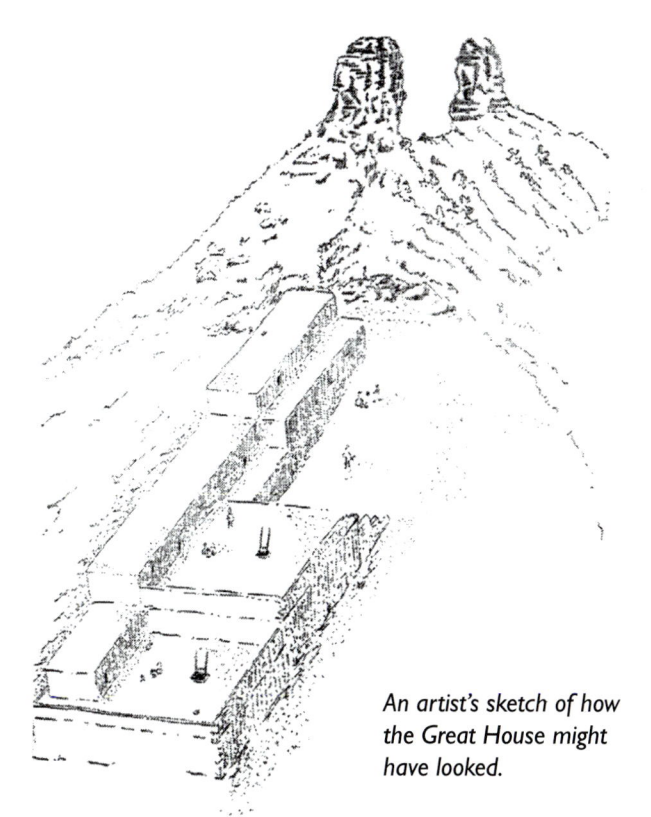

An artist's sketch of how the Great House might have looked.

Illustration from Chimney Rock Volunteer Handbook

This theory paints a dramatic picture of Chimney Rock as a possible moon shrine—its Great House built to celebrate the event. Perhaps it was built to welcome pilgrims and skywatchers from all over the Four Corners region to observe this cycle of moon risings. The culmination of each cycle, the rising of the full moon at sunset in the cold of December,

Visions of Chimney Rock

could have been the high point of nearly two decades of preparation and study for the Ancestral Puebloans.

We almost certainly will never know if this theory depicts reality. Some evidence supports the theory.

Whatever the reason for building and living at this complex site, it was not to last. Just as we'll never know all we want to know about this ancient culture, it also will remain a mystery why the Ancestral Puebloans left the site.

The departure

Around AD 1125, based on pottery style changes, the people left Chimney Rock for reasons we can only guess. From AD 1080 to about AD 1100, the climate had become progressively drier, probably stressing this agricultural community. The powerful Chaco Canyon culture was breaking down about this time and its outliers were falling silent across the region. If Chimney Rock was, in fact, an astronomical shrine or solar observatory, a total solar eclipse in AD 1097 may have been seen as an unfavorable omen.

Did the culture fade or the land play out? We'll never know with certainty why the Ancestral Puebloans left Chimney Rock.

Photo by Helen L. Richardson

CHAPTER 3: The Place

After painstakingly constructing the Great House from nearly six million stones, the Ancestral Puebloans walked away from their masterpiece.
Photo courtesy of the US Forest Service, Pagosa District

There may not have been any single overarching cause for leaving. Perhaps the land simply played out and could no longer produce food. Perhaps a combination of changing climate, overpopulation, hunger, social change, bad omens, and competition from other tribes proved too much for this small village.

Where did the people go? No one knows, but some possibly went west to Mesa Verde, some south to Chaco Canyon, some to the pueblos of Taos and the Tewa-speaking San Juan, Santa Clara, San Ildefonso, Pojoaque, Nambe, and Tesuque. Chimney-Rock-style pottery has been found in New Mexico sites such as Gobernador, Gallina, and Bandelier, which were deserted later than Chimney Rock.

The modern Pueblo people of Taos and the Tewa-speaking pueblos may be descendants of the people of Chimney Rock. Some elders claim

Visions of Chimney Rock

they originated in the area of the twin pinnacles. This is certainly a real possibility since these pueblos began during the same time frame.

After occupying the high mesa for hundreds of years, the Ancestral Puebloans moved on.

Photo courtesy of the US Forest Service, Pagosa District

It seems logical the Ancestral Puebloans, faced with a collapse of their way of life, might have sought out people of similar cultures for aid and security. The similarities between the Ancestral Puebloans and

CHAPTER 3: The Place

some of the modern pueblos across northern New Mexico are strong arguments for a cultural link. The multi-dwelling adobe structures, the stone construction, the style and technology of the ceramics all add weight to the case. Archaeological evidence does not link Chimney Rock to the Zuni and Hopi people, although both groups incorporate features in their cultures similar to some found at Chimney Rock and other pre-pueblo structures.

The structures and artifacts left behind in the Chimney Rock Archaeological Area offer a glimpse into the lives of the Ancestral Puebloans who lived and worked on the high mesa beneath Chimney Rock. The stone pinnacles themselves offer a much clearer record of their own origin.

CHAPTER FOUR

The Rocks

Visions of Chimney Rock

Nature at work

Long before the Ancestral Puebloans built their homes in the shadow of Chimney Rock, the stone towers were formed by incredible forces of nature.

Photo by Jeff Laydon

Eons of time and climatic conditions—and perhaps serendipity—worked together to form the two stone pinnacles we know today as Chimney Rock and Companion Rock. Their story begins at least a hundred million years ago when the land that today basks in the shadow of high peaks was covered by a vast sea.

Long before humans found the mesa and spires of Chimney Rock, this impressive landmark was created by the forces of nature. Over millions of years, mud slowly settled in the shallow sea, building layers nearly two thousand feet deep. Animals and plants lived and died and were entombed in the soft ooze, leaving evidence of their forms and the environment in which they lived.

CHAPTER 4: The Rocks

The creatures of the vast ocean left myriad marks on the formations that followed their demise.

Photo by L. Larason for the US Forest Service

This incredible work of time and the elements continued to change. The North American continent moved west, driven by deep currents in the earth's semi-molten interior, and was carried over a hot spot—an immense upwelling of molten rock. The heat stretched and raised the earth's crust, building the peaks of the Rocky Mountains. As the land was lifted, the ocean drained away to the south. The shoreline, with its beaches, tidal flats, and river deltas, followed the ocean's edge, laying down a thick layer of sand and silt over the ancient ocean mud. Forests and swamps followed in turn, built by wandering rivers and their flood plains and backwaters. The Dinosaur Age was in its last flower, and shoals of clams and oysters added their shells to the sediment alongside the bones of the great beasts. Trees fell, swamps flooded and drained, and a vast layer of fossil-bearing sediments and coal seams formed above the sandy beaches of the buried shoreline.

After the end of the Dinosaur Age, about 65 million years ago, volcanic eruptions devastated the forests and swamps and piled up mountains that rivaled today's Rockies. Thick layers of debris, eroded from the new

Visions of Chimney Rock

volcanoes, piled up and buried the dead forests and built new landscapes in a cycle that lasted for tens of millions of years. Some ten million years ago the volcanoes began to die, robbed of their force as the continent moved past the hot spot beneath. The dead volcanoes continued to erode, shedding huge blankets of rock and soil into the rivers. Only a few million years ago, rolling hills and large river valleys sloped and drained into the San Juan Basin to the south.

The oldest rocks at Chimney Rock, the gray shales at the foot of the mesa slopes, are thought to be about 90 million years old, only one fifth of one percent of the earth's age.

Photo by L. Larason for the US Forest Service

Then the earth spiraled into a Glacial Age. Cool, wet summers and icy winters ruled this part of Colorado. Glaciers further sculpted the land, scouring the sides of mountains and valleys, pouring broken rock, sand, and clay into raging torrents of melt water. The tilted layers of ancient sea bed, shoreline, beaches, swamps, and river deposits were attacked by these floods of melt water and carried away.

CHAPTER 4: The Rocks

Today, snow is a rarity on Chimney Rock where once giant glaciers contributed to their formation.

Photo by Helen L. Richardson

The spires appear

About one hundred thousand years ago, erosion at what is now Chimney Rock finally exposed a thick, deep sand layer, probably the bed of an ancient river that once coursed to the southwest. This layer was hard, and resisted the erosion of the nearby flood-swollen stream today known as the Piedra River.

Seeking the easiest path, the river looped around this high ground, leaving a long, narrow ridge of sandstone perched on the much softer shale beneath it. The melting glaciers faded away and, just twelve thousand years in the past, the climate warmed into an interglacial period. Human beings began exploring and colonizing this newly ice-free land. The mammoths and mastodons, the giant sloths, and the American lion, horse, camel, and many other beasts of the Ice Age began to disappear.

Even after the ancient oceans drained away, it took millennia of time to carve the spectacular towers from the surrounding stone.

Photo by David Herrell

No longer fed by melting rivers of glacial ice, the shrunken Piedra River relinquished its erosive grip on the long, narrow spine of sandstone. But nature still attacked with freezing winters and shattering heat in summer, with wind-driven sandblasting, and perhaps the tremors of earthquakes. While parts of the wall of rock gradually cracked and fell away, two towers of stone remain. They stand atop a narrow remnant of that ancient river bed, looking down on a fertile valley at the foot of the Rocky Mountains, dividing the deserts of the south from the cold, high peaks of the Continental Divide.

And so, sometime between 1,200 and 1,500 years ago, people found Chimney Rock—a land where layers of fine-grained shale sandwich thin beds of sandstone, rising in steep slopes from the adobe mud of the valley floor—the bed of a vanished ocean. This thick, narrow mesa of

CHAPTER 4: The Rocks

sandstone is dotted with fossil leaves and plant stems, layered with the ripples of tidal seas, the burrows of sand crabs from the ancient shore and beaches that succeeded the ocean.

Rising above all else are the twin pillars of stone, carved from the bed of a vanished river, now the landmark for a human culture that has also vanished. Like the story told by the fossils and rocks, the story of Chimney Rock's people can only be read from pieces that were left behind.

Interpreting these relics may be the work of professionals, but each summer a cadre of dedicated volunteers introduces growing numbers of visitors to the story of Chimney Rock and its people as we know it.

In 1776, Spanish missionaries and Dominguez Escalante named the river El Rio de la Piedra Parado, River of the Standing Rocks, even though they likely never saw the stone towers themselves.

Photo by Dick Moseley

Visions of Chimney Rock

The top of Chimney Rock is at 7,900 feet elevation, reaching 300 feet above the mesa top and almost 1,300 feet above the valley floor.

Photo by John G. Richardson

CHAPTER FIVE

Chimney Rock Today

Visions of Chimney Rock

Plan for the future

The 4,100-acre Chimney Rock Archaeological Area includes many un-excavated Ancestral Puebloan sites.
Photo by L. Larason for the US Forest Service

The growing desire to understand Native American cultures by the American people led to a move to preserve Chimney Rock's Ancestral Puebloan structures. Throughout the late 1950s and early 1960s, letters to state and national legislators, publicity campaigns in local and regional media, and plans by the Forest Service and the Southern Ute Indian Tribe centered on the stone pillars and their surroundings. In 1968, Dr. Frank Eddy took over the systematic re-investigation of the area. He documented and refined most of Jeançon's and Roberts' earlier work, surveyed and excavated new sites, and directed stabilization work.

By 1970, with Eddy's active support, the US Forest Service created a development plan and designed and funded Chimney Rock, adding to the Four Corners area's Ancestral Puebloan cultural settings. An area of 3,160 acres was designated the Chimney Rock Archaeological Area. A core of 960 acres, including the spires and the high mesa's spectacular pueblo ruins and village site, was listed on the National Register of Historic Places. Currently, the protected area encompasses 4,100 acres.

As part of the US Forest Service development plan, Eddy directed a crew of expert Navajo masons from the Chaco Culture National Historical Park as they began the process of stabilizing Chimney Rock's ancient buildings. This involved the selective and careful reconstruction

CHAPTER 5: Chimney Rock Today

Excavation and stabilization of the Great House were under way in 1972.

   Historic photo courtesy of the US Forest Service, Pagosa District

Visions of Chimney Rock

and strengthening of the ruins to withstand the extremes of weather and to make them accessible to visitors without undue damage to the site. The major excavation and stabilization work centered on the Great Kiva, the Pit House, the Ridge House, the Guard House, and the Great House Pueblo.

The development of the Chimney Rock Archaeological Area was under way but received an unexpected interruption. In 1974, a pair of peregrine falcons was discovered nesting on the stone pillars. At the time, the falcons were an endangered species. Therefore, the protection of the falcons and their nesting location took precedence over recreational development of the new Archaeological Area.

Illustrations by Dick Ostergaard

The construction and stabilization work was halted and a period of study begun to determine what impact tourism would have on the nesting birds. An area of one mile in diameter, centered on the two rock spires, was closed to all entry and use until the study could be completed.

Protect and study

Until the 1980s, the Chimney Rock Archaeological Area was essentially closed except for irregular tours conducted by the Forest Service, and little study was accomplished. Forest Service Archaeologist Robert York supervised the protection of the site and conducted limited public and professional tours. Later, the falcons abandoned the spires as a nesting site and, despite efforts to reintroduce them, no falcons returned to Chimney Rock until the mid-1990s.

CHAPTER 5: Chimney Rock Today

It took a team effort to open the Chimney Rock Archaeological Area to the public.
Photo by Helen L. Richardson

By that time, demand for visitor access was growing and a recovery plan for the peregrine falcons was designed to allow limited tourism while preserving the wild nature of the nesting place.

Local residents formed the Friends of Chimney Rock to promote protection and enjoyment of the site. This group of volunteers conducted tours and gave educational presentations about Chimney Rock.

Over the years, the Friends of Chimney Rock have merged with educational non-profit groups. Today, the group is the independent Chimney Rock Interpretive Association (CRIA).

Visions of Chimney Rock

Volunteer tour guides and cabin hosts support the Chimney Rock Interpretive Program with thousands of hours of their time.
Photo courtesy of the US Forest Service, Pagosa District

Volunteers make it work

CRIA operates an interpretive program at Chimney Rock staffed by an outstanding volunteer program. Upwards of sixty volunteers participate as tour guides, cabin hosts, upkeep stewards, and in various other capacities each season, donating thousands of hours of their time to keep the program alive and share the story of Chimney Rock with at least 11,000 visitors in the summer.

In an effort to bring increased reality to the interpretive program, volunteers and crafts people demonstrate ancient tools and crafts at an annual Life at Chimney Rock day. Visitors may make a pot, throw a spear using an atlatl, watch an expert flint knapper create hand tools, pound

CHAPTER 5: Chimney Rock Today

yucca leaves to release their fibers, carve their own petroglyphs (stone art), grind corn with stones called manos and metates, watch an expert spin yarn from dog hair using a drop spindle, or even participate in a pottery workshop using 1,000-year-old techniques.

A young visitor to Life at Chimney Rock tries her hand at pounding yucca.
Photo by Helen L. Richardson

The Chimney Rock Interpretive Program reaches out to schoolchildren throughout the region.
Photo courtesy of the US Forest Service, Pagosa District

Visions of Chimney Rock

Young fingers shape a small pot as the Ancestral Puebloans may have done a thousand years ago.
Photo by Helen L. Richardson

An experienced volunteer shows visitors how the Ancestral Puebloans used a simple drop spindle to spin dog hair into yarn.
Photo by Helen L. Richardson

CHAPTER 5: Chimney Rock Today

Sunset color lights the rocks before the spectacular appearance of the moon.

Photo by John G. Richardson

As many as 150 visitors climb the mesa each month to watch the full moon rise over distant mountains.

Photo courtesy of the US Forest Service, Pagosa District

Visions of Chimney Rock

Each month during the summer, volunteers light the trail to the mesa top for a full moon program beneath the twin spires. Speakers tell the story of the people and their likely relationship with the moon and sun and stars as they watch the full moon rise over the eastern mountain peaks.

Return of native cultures

Hopi Dancers were among the first Native Americans to bring their social dances to Chimney Rock.

Photo used with permission of Eldon Kewanyama

Beginning in 1995, Native Americans once again brought their drumbeats and mystical flute music to Chimney Rock. Through a non-profit organization known as Friends of Native Cultures, visitors to Chimney Rock have enjoyed presentations of traditional music, song, dance, and storytelling from numerous Native American people. Presenting groups include Hopi, Zuni, Yaqui, Aztec, Southern Ute, and Ute Mountain Ute people as well as representatives from the pueblos of Taos, San Juan, Santa Clara, Acoma, Laguna, and Picuris. These traditional presentations

CHAPTER 5: Chimney Rock Today

give the public an opportunity to envision how the site might have been used centuries ago. For many of the presenters, it's a deeply spiritual occasion, a return to their roots, a chance to commune with the spirits of their ancestors.

Nearly a thousand years of sunrises and sunsets have not revealed all the secrets of the Ancestral Puebloans who made their homes within sight of Chimney Rock.

Photo by Bruce Andersen

Excavation, stabilization, and study of the site are ongoing by Forest Service Archaeologists and other scientists. Research, excavation, new concepts and interpretations are what make archaeology a dynamic science. No definitive answer is ever likely to satisfy those who study Chimney Rock. We can set out the known facts and many of the ideas based on those facts but, in the end, we can only wonder why the people made their homes on the high mesa beneath Chimney Rock and Companion Rock and what significance they gave to the twin spires.

Acknowledgements

This book has been begging to be published for as many years as volunteers have loved the Chimney Rock Archaeological Area. *Visions of Chimney Rock* does not pretend to be an exhaustive treatise of the Ancestral Puebloan habitation at Chimney Rock. For those who wish to learn more, there is an extensive bibliography.

While I get to put my name on the cover as editor, many creative, knowledgable people have contributed valuable resources to make this book a reality. The experts whose knowledge supplied the narrative were the first essential ingredient. The decision to make it a factual picture book rather than simply text made way for the input of many skilled photographers who donated use of their images. In addition to the two talented illustrators who receive credit, and whom we deeply appreciate, we owe a debt of gratitude to the unnamed sketch artists who have, over the years, contributed the detailed illustrations used in the Chimney Rock Volunteer Handbook. I especially appreciate the attention to detail of Ann Graves and Sepp Ramsperger who proofread the manuscript. Finally, the folks who helped raise the money to actually bring it to print deserve special thanks. And I am deeply indebted to Glenn Raby, Gary Fairchild, and Jo Bridges for their unflagging support and encouragement.

Helen L. Richardson, editor

Special thanks to:
The Ballantine Family Charitable Fund
The Chimney Rock Interpretive Association
The United Methodist Church of Pagosa Springs

Bibliography

Archaeological Research of Southwestern Colorado. "Archaeological Research in the Northeastern San Juan Basin of Colorado During the Summer of 1921." Denver, CO: The State Historical and Natural History Society of Colorado and the University of Denver.

Dunmire, William W. and Gail D. Tierney, *Wild Plants and Native Peoples of the Four Corners.* Santa Fe, NM: Museum of New Mexico Press, 1997.

Photo courtesy of the US Forest Service, Pagosa District

Eddy, Frank W. "Archaeological Investigations at Chimney Rock Mesa, 1970-1972." Boulder, CO: Colorado Archaeological Society, 1977.

Eddy, Frank W. "Final Archaeological Report Covering Research at the Chimney Rock Mesa, 1977-1982." Durango, CO: Manuscript on file, San Juan National Forest-Supervisor's Office.

Ellis, Florence M. and J.J. Brody. "Ceramic Stratigraphy and Tribal History at Taos Pueblo." Vol. 29: No. 3 of *American Antiquity*. 1964, pp. 316-327.

Ford, Richard, Albert H. Schroeder, and Stewart L. Peckham. "Three Perspectives of Pueblo Prehistory." Edited by Alfonso Ortiz. In *Perspectives on the Pueblos,* pp. 22-44. Albuquerque, NM: University of New Mexico Press, 1972.

Gabriel, Kathryn. *Roads to Center Place*. Boulder, CO: Johnson Books, 1991.

Hatch, Sharon. "A Wood Sourcing Study at the Chimney Rock Archaeological Area Southwest Colorado." Thesis prospectus submitted to the Department of Anthropology, Northern Arizona University, Feb. 26, 1993. This paper contains an extensive bibliography of valuable sources.

Hawthorne, Bill. Draft handbook manuscript. Copy held in Pagosa Ranger District Office.

Houle, Mary Cottrell. *Wings For My Flight: The Peregrine Falcons of Chimney Rock.* Reading, MA: Addison-Wesley, 1991.

Jeançon, Jean A. and Frank H. H. Roberts, Jr. "Further Archaeological Research in the Northeastern San Juan Basin of Colorado During the Summer of 1922." Vol. 1: No. 2 and Vol. 1: No. 3 of *The Colorado Magazine.*

Judge, W. James. "The Development of a Complex Cultural Ecosystem in the Chaco Basin, New Mexico." In Proceedings of the First Conference on Scientific Research in the National Parks, 3, edited by R. M. Linn, pp. 901-906. National Park Service Transactions and Proceedings, Series 5: Washington, DC, 1979.

Kane, Allen. "Organizational Models for Northern Chacoan Outlier Communities." Paper prepared for the Third Anasazi Conference: Monument Valley, AZ, Oct. 10, 1986.

Kershaw, Linda. *Edible and Medicinal Plants of the Rockies.* Edmonton, Alberta, Canada: Lone Pine Publishing, 2000.

Lekson, Stephen H.; J. McKim Malville; Frank W. Eddy; Douglas R. Parker; Mary Sullivan; Gordon C. Tucker, Jr.; Allen E. Kane; Bruce Bradley; W. James Judge; David Wilcox; and John R. Roney, *Chimney Rock: The Ultimate Outlier.* Boulder, CO: Lexington Books, 2005.

Lister, Florence C. *In the Shadow of the Rockies.* Boulder, CO: University Press of Colorado, 1993.

BIBLIOGRAPHY

Photo by Helen L. Richardson

Lister, Robert H. and Florence C. Lister. *Anasazi Pottery*. Albuquerque, NM: University of New Mexico Press, 1968.

Malville, J. McKim, and Claudia Putnam. *Prehistoric Astronomy in the Southwest*. Boulder, CO: Johnson Books, 1989.

Malville, J. McKim, and Gary Matlock, Editors. "The Chimney Rock Archaeological Symposium." Collection of papers written by symposium attendees, 1990, USDA Forest Service General Technical Report RM-227: Fort Lewis College, Durango, CO, 1993.

Matlock, Gary. *Enemy Ancestors*. Flagstaff, AZ: Northland Press, 1988.

Powers, Robert P. "Regional Interaction in the San Juan Basin: The Chaco Outlier System." In *Recent Research on Chaco Canyon Prehistory*, edited by W. James Judge and John D. Schelburg. Albuquerque, NM: Reports of the Chaco Center No. 8, Division of Cultural Research, National Park Service, 1984.

Roberts, Frank H. H.. "Report on an Archaeological Reconnaissance in Southwestern Colorado in the Summer of 1923." *The Colorado Magazine*, pp 2-80, April, 1925.

Vivian, R. Gwinn. *The Chacoan Prehistory of the San Juan Basin.* New York: Academic Press, 1990.

Windes, Thomas C. *Stone Circles of Chaco Canyon.* Albuquerque, NM: NW New Mexico, 1978.

Index

alignment, 81, 87
alignments, 87, 88
Anasazi, 9, 16
Anasazi Heritage Center, 6
Ancestral Puebloan, 2, 9, 10, 14, 15, 16, 18, 39, 42, 55, 68, 84, 92, 104
archaeoastronomy, 13, 70, 83
Archaic Indians, 7
astronomy, 82
atlatl, 36, 108
Aztec Ruins, 54, 65, 78

Basketmaker, 9, 21, 36
Basketmaker II, 36
bow and arrow, 36

catchment system, 63
Chaco Canyon, 13, 40, 49, 56, 65, 68, 75, 81, 91
Chaco Culture National Historical Park, 104
Chacoan architecture, 13, 65
Chacoan culture, 13, 14, 39, 42, 65, 69, 90
Chacoan influence, 65
Chacoan occupation, 66
Chacoan outlier, 65, 68, 90
Chacoan roads, 39, 62
check dams, 27
Chimney Rock, 2, 10, 12, 13, 14, 22, 42, 63, 65, 69, 75, 84, 85, 89, 90, 96, 99, 100

Chimney Rock Archaeological Area, 59, 93, 104, 106
Chimney Rock Phase, 14
chinking, 73, 81
clothing, 20
Companion Rock, 2, 70, 84, 85, 96
construction types
    daub and wattle, 8
    jacal, 8, 43, 59
    pit house, 46
Crab Nebula, 83
cribbed-roof, 78

dating methods
    pottery styles, 82
    stratigraphy, 44, 50
    tree-ring dating, 50, 82, 86
dendrochronology, 44
Denver University Museum, 6
departure, 90, 91
Dinosaur Age, 97
drop spindle, 109
dry-land plots, 27
dual governance, 18, 77

Eddy, Frank, 14, 36, 37, 46, 77, 78, 81, 104
equinox, 57, 84
Escalante Ruin, 65

fire lookout tower, 76, 80
fire pit, 47, 53, 61

121

food sources, 28
  beans, 9, 25, 49
  corn, 7, 25, 49, 55, 109
  game, 5
  gathering, 7, 26
  hunting, 7, 26
  maize, 9, 25, 27
  squash, 7
foot drum, 53
Forest Service, 12, 104, 106, 108, 111, 114
Four Corners, 2, 4, 7, 9, 10, 65, 104
Friends of Chimney Rock, 107
Friends of Native Cultures, 112

geology, 95
Glacial Age, 98
Great House, 12, 43, 44, 56, 57, 62, 63, 65, 68, 69, 71, 73, 77, 81, 84, 85, 86, 106
Great Kiva, 44, 51, 54, 56, 75, 106, 112
Guard House, 40, 44, 63, 65, 106

Halley's Comet, 83
hammer stones, 49
Hohokam, 7, 21
Hopi, 16, 64
Huerfano Mesa, 2, 68

Ice Age, 100
irrigation, 27

Jeançon, Jean Allard, 14, 37, 40, 49, 62, 65, 73, 74, 77, 78, 104

kiva religion, 55

language
  Keres, 15
  Tanoan, 15
  Tewa, 15
  Tiwa, 15
life at Chimney Rock, 108
lunar observatory, 3, 13, 70, 83
lunar standstill, 70, 78, 84, 86

Malville, Dr. J. McKim, 57, 85
mano, 25, 49, 61, 109
Mesa Verde, 13, 14, 22, 78, 91
metate, 25, 49, 61, 71, 109
midden, 22
Mogollon, 7, 21
moities, 77
Montezuma Basin, 49
Museum of Natural History, 6

Navajo, 16, 30, 32, 34, 104

olla, 37
ornaments, 20
Ortiz, Dr. Alfonso, 55

Paleo Indian, 4
peregrine falcons, 106, 107
Peterson Mesa, 84
petroglyph, 15, 109
pictograph, 15
Piedra Phase, 14
Piedra River, 2, 10, 14, 27, 37, 43, 56, 84, 99, 100
Pit House, 16, 44, 48, 49, 50, 51, 59, 62, 106

INDEX

pottery, 21
    black-on-white, 22
    Mancos Corrugated, 23
    Payan Corrugated, 23
    Plain Gray, 23
prayer plume holders, 49, 58
Pueblo I, 21, 82
Pueblo II, 21, 60, 82
Pueblo III, 21, 82

Ridge House, 44, 60, 61, 106
Roberts, Frank H.H., Jr., 14, 38, 40, 62, 74, 77, 104
Rocky Mountains, 97, 100
Room 8, 81

Salmon Ruins, 65
Salvage Site, 44, 59
San Juan Basin, 98
San Juan Mountains Association, 121

San Juan River, 10
Sinagua, 21
skywatchers, 55, 57, 82
solar eclipse, 83, 90
solar observatory, 3, 13, 70, 83, 84
Southern Ute Tribe, 104
stone basin, 56, 84
summer solstice, 84
Sun Tower, 55, 89
supernova, 83
symmetry, 77

trade networks, 21

useful plants
    Banana Yucca, 29
    Chokecherry, 30
    Cholla, 33
    Claret Cup Cactus, 31
    Cliff Fendlerbush, 30

Photo by Helen L. Richardson

Penstemon, 32
Rabbitbrush, 29
Ricegrass, 34
Rocky Mountain Beeplant, 22
Simpson's Ball Cactus, 31
Snowberry, 33
Sunflower, 33
Wyoming Paintbrush, 32

ventilator system, 47, 61
volunteers, 101, 107, 108, 112

Wallace Ruin, 49
winter solstice, 57, 84, 85

York, Robert, 106
yucca, 19, 20, 24, 36, 109
Yucca House, 65

Zuni, 16